ROOTS
&
ROUTES

Randy G. Litchfield

ROOTS & ROUTES

Calling, Ministry, and the Power of Place

Abingdon Press™

Nashville

ROOTS AND ROUTES:
Calling, Ministry, and the Power of Place

Copyright © 2019 by Abingdon Press

This book is printed on acid-free paper.

Library of Congress Cataloging-in-Publication Data has been requested.

ISBN 978-1-5018-6815-3

19 20 21 22 23 24 25 26 27—10 9 8 7 6 5 4 3 2 1
MANUFACTURED IN THE UNITED STATES OF AMERICA

CONTENTS

ACKNOWLEDGMENTS

I have many people to thank on the routes to this book. First, to Terri Litchfield, who is a supportive and patient partner in the places and routes of my life. Space does not permit me to thank the host of persons in congregations, schools, and workplaces who have taught, mentored, and guided me. I am very grateful for the feedback on drafts of this manuscript from Jack Seymour, Lisa Withrow, Linda Ogden, Margaret Ann Crain, Norma Cook Everist, Wendy Bartlett, and Jacqui Buschor. The students of PT500 Leadership, Learning and Community Formation and PT640 Knowing Where We Dwell at Methodist Theological School in Ohio (MTSO), of whom Wendy and Jacqui were a part, advanced my thinking and development of this project. So did members of Asbury United Methodist Church (Delaware, Ohio) who participated in a six-week educational program based on the book. I am thankful for the year-long sabbatical fellowship allowed by the trustees and faculty of MTSO during which much of this project was developed. Finally, I wish to thank David Teel (a former editor at Abingdon Press who took a chance on my proposal and supported the development of my work) and Michael Stephens (my current editor at Abingdon who guided the project through final editing). Along with David and Michael, I am indebted to the careful and helpful work of Laurie Vaughen, my production editor, and copy editor Jennifer Veilleux at Abingdon Press.

PREFACE

This book brings together two themes in my journey. One is the notion of vocation and the other is engagement with context. The vocational theme emerged as I began part-time seminary classes while an engineer at a division of General Motors. The struggle to discern personal vocation in that period shaped the goals and designs of courses I taught over the years with undergraduate and seminary students. The contextual theme grew as I learned about enculturation, ethnography, and issues of diversity as part of educational systems and practical theology. Eventually the concept of place overtook context as a way for me to understand local relationships and situations, because place encompasses human and nonhuman dimensions of the world. Place is a way to concretely engage intersectionality in a comprehensive manner. Vocation and place converged in my thinking as I read Mary McClintock Fulkerson's *Places of Redemption: Theology for a Worldly Church*.[1] I was struck by her treatment of places as situations that evoke a response in us and it seemed to me such responses are partnerships with God and particular embodiments of vocation—hence place evokes vocation.[2]

When teaching undergraduates, I frequently heard their deep desires to make a difference in the world. I continue to encounter that desire now as I work with seminary students whether or not they are seeking ordination. There are many critiques of the contemporary church and explanations for why the church, as well as many theological schools, in the US are in decline. Blame is put on institutionalism, traditionalism, loss of mission, ineffective leadership, uncommitted laity, organizational dysfunction, wars over worship style, theological relativism, and (yes) theological education. For many, including the spiritual but nor religious (SBNR) who are found inside as well as beyond congregations,[3] the question of involvement in a congregation is not if religion makes sense but whether it makes a difference—to their spirituality, well-being, relationships, community and society. As Jack Seymour writes,

> We already know what makes a congregation vital—it is changed lives. It is places where new life is present when brokenness seems the reality, where grace offers new chances, where healing occurs, where communities are reborn and reshaped.[4]

Perhaps my theology of human nature is a bit optimistic, but the desire to make a difference seems pervasive. At the same time, I recognize that church leaders bemoan rampant apathy and the necessity to find ways to motivate people to become involved. The things that many church leaders go through to fill committees and find volunteers for ministries! This raises important questions. What contributes to persons drifting from a desire to make a difference to apathy and disengagement? What passivates people of faith? How does vocation become disconnected from discipleship? There is no simple answer to such questions, but I am confident that part of the solution is fostering rich vocational imagination and embracing the interdependence between vocation and place.

The roots and routes of my life shape this book. In terms of social location, I am a straight white Protestant male. I grew up in Anderson, Indiana, which was once a smallish industrial town but with the decline of the auto industry is now economically depressed. My parents were of the "Great Generation" with only high school educations and our economic status was blue-collar. Through childhood and youth I was active in a Disciples of Christ congregation. In college I studied mechanical engineering and I spent a significant amount of time in Catholic parishes at school and home. After graduation I became more involved with my home Disciples of Christ congregation, helping with the youth program. Feeling inadequate for this work, I took the suggestion of Scott Luppe, our youth minister, and took classes at Anderson University School of Theology while working full time as a project engineer at Delco Remy (then a division of General Motors). Shortly after starting seminary I met Terri, my wife, and became associated with the Church of God (Anderson, Indiana)—the tradition of Terri and the seminary. By the time I finished my Masters in Religious Education, all the discernment and feedback led me to leave GM and do a PhD in Theology and Personality with a specialization in religious education at Claremont School of Theology. I was immersed in issues of diversity, process theology, practical theology, liberative approaches to education, and congregational studies. While in Claremont our daughter, Erin, was born and we worshiped in a UCC congregation. After Claremont, I returned to Anderson University and taught in the undergraduate program for nine years and while there re-associated with the Church of God. We later moved to central Ohio so I could join the faculty of Methodist Theological School in Ohio and became a United Methodist. During my time at MTSO, I served five years as academic dean. I remain a layperson.

This book is intended for those preparing for, or already engaged in, some form of leadership related to faith communities. It brings together education, leadership, and practical theology. In religiously affiliated undergraduate settings, the book resources general education courses addressing vocation and classes related to ministry majors. In graduate theological education the book could be used in introductory leadership, education, or practical theology courses. In communities of faith, the book resources clergy, professional, and lay leadership who are interested in empowering individuals and their communities in service to the world. Some adult studies might effectively use the book to explore vocation and place.

I hope this book aids persons in their spiritual dwelling and journeying. Some possibilities include the following:

> For those wanting to make a difference in the world, nurture a rich imagination of ways to be in vocation in the many places and paths of life

For those feeling that they "missed their calling" or their calling has ended, offer hope in the understanding that vocation is an ongoing process rather than something to possess

For those longing for humanity *and* creation to flourish, provide place as an approach to the intersections of brokenness and giftedness

For those burdened by compartmentalized understandings of ministry, offer a view of vocation based on place and partnership that bridges ordained, professional, and lay categories

For those seeking encounter and partnership with God, propose incarnational ways of engaging the places and routes of life

For those in theological education and congregations tasked with forming the next generation of church leaders, suggest ways to prepare persons for dynamic and varied forms of vocation in across the places and paths of life

—Randy G. Litchfield

Chapter 1
PURPOSE, PLACE, AND VOCATIONAL IMAGINATION

"IT WAS A GREAT EXPERIENCE; IT WAS A TERRIBLE EXPERIENCE...."

When I tell stories about vocation in my life, they are often punctuated by the refrain, "It was a great experience; it was a terrible experience." I earned a Bachelor of Science degree in mechanical engineering from a college with a General Motors–related co-op program that had students alternating each twelve weeks between school and our sponsoring division, which in my case was located in my hometown. College included some religious searching. I almost became Roman Catholic, and I spent some time in a Nazarene congregation, but whenever home, I attended our Disciples of Christ congregation with Mom. After graduation, I continued to work for my sponsoring division as a product engineer. I started getting more involved at church, volunteering as a youth group assistant and becoming good friends with the part-time youth minister, Scott. That first summer Scott invited me to join him as counselor for a weeklong fifth- and sixth-grade church summer camp. "It was a great experience; it was a terrible experience." I enjoyed working with the kids, but ultimately, I felt so clueless as to what I was doing or how to just talk about faith.

Shortly after, following Scott's advice, I enrolled as a part-time, non-degree student in two classes at the seminary in town. One class was on ministry with children, and the other was an introduction to the Synoptic Gospels taught by Dr. James Earl Massey. "It was a great experience; it was a terrible experience." The classes were wonderful—I learned both content and new ways of seeing the world. I also felt so out of place in class—I was sure I was a sinner among saintly seminarians...an imposter.

Work was going well, and I was thinking about doing an MBA to prepare for corporate advancement, but work was also straining and draining. Volunteer ministry at the church was satisfying and my youth minister friend was mentoring me, but I was uneasy about what might lie ahead. Did these "great and terrible" experiences mean I was facing "the call" to formal church ministry? Surely not! Preaching, evangelism, visitations...these do not mix with a self-conscious introvert. Yet something was happening. I met and married Terri, the love of my life. I enrolled part-time in the Master of Religious Education degree program, taking two classes a semester while continuing to work as an engineer. I became associated with the Church of God (Anderson, Indiana), the denomination of the seminary, and was very involved in church ministries.

I was grappling with a doggedly stubborn question of vocation. It presented itself most forcefully in terms of career but rippled through many aspects and places of my life. All I could imagine was formal ministry. Terri married an engineer, not a pastor. Our household economics might be put on the line. Was I being called to be a pastor or just a well-prepared layperson in a congregation? Was that even an option? Increasingly my identity was amorphous, hyphenated to connect the place I was at the time with other places of identity. Was I a seminarian-engineer, an engineer-seminarian, a seminarian-congregant, or something I could not express? This particular season of vocational discernment stretched a two-year degree into six and saw me become a product development team leader. Many of the things I studied about learning, groups, and community contributed to the role of team leader. Apart from the accumulating burnout, was I having a great experience—or did it qualify as another terrible experience?

At the end of my MRE, clarity about pursuing academics coincided with separation incentives offered by GM. I took the opportunity to earn my PhD in Theology and Personality (Religious Education) and then taught at Anderson University and now at Methodist Theological School in Ohio.

In working with undergraduates and seminarians, I resonate with the ups and downs I hear in their stories about the journey of faith and about finding a place of purpose—a place of vocation. Several themes in recognizing and living into one's vocation emerge from these stories. One theme is the challenge of finding identity—who am I in the midst of various places, roles, and formative relationships? A second theme is interpreting experiences of satisfaction and difficulty—what are my animating passions? A third theme is facing fears of taking risks and facing self-doubt—am I sure enough about my calling to act upon it? A fourth theme is limiting vocation to certain roles (such as pastor) and certain places (like the church). Young adulthood is the stereotypical season of life to be sorting out issues of identity, purpose, and belonging. But the reality is that identity, purpose, and belonging are continually evolving throughout life, whether subtly or vastly.

This chapter begins the project of exploring these and other themes in the hope of fostering robust vocation in the places and on routes of life. Our starting point is the interplay of identity, vocation, and place. The nature of our identities is narrative. We construct our identities through the stories we tell about ourselves, and we do that by drawing upon the stories we find in the places and routes of our lives. Identity is also closely connected to vocation. Vocation projects a sense of what our story is about—where the storyline of our identity is heading. Additionally, vocation and identity come together as a sense of whose we are and with whom we partner—belonging to God, places, and routes. I suggest that many struggles with embracing vocation emerge from failed vocational imagination—imagination that is limited in scope and disconnected from the places and routes of life. This chapter ends with a sketch of a more robust vocational imagination.

THE STORIED SELF AND PLACE

The nature of human experience is narrative.[1] It is a way of understanding the self as episodic and fluid, while still having some degree of coherence. Our telling and retelling of life experiences through narratives is a process of becoming ourselves. With each retelling, there is a re-valuing of moments of experience and that retelling can be either destructive or redemptive. The moments of experience are ours, but we do not create the storylines connecting them *ex nihilo*. We draw from narrative patterns from the communities and places where we find ourselves, blending them into our self-understanding with a mix of conformity, novelty, and even hostility.

For example, when I was working at GM, I drew upon storylines of corporate culture about being an engineer. At home, the storylines were of my family of origin and about being a spouse. At church, the storylines were of being a Christian. I interjected novelty into the storyline of engineer, tried to reject parts of inherited spousal storylines, and largely adopted storylines of being Christian. There is no lack of resources for creating the stories of self. We encounter the storylines of the variety of places in which we move in daily life and over the course of our life-span. Additionally, each place we dwell and move holds many storylines. Some predominate and some are muted; some are liberating and some are entrapping.

In Christian faith communities, testimonies of faith, faith journeys, and call stories provide good examples of what I am describing. Each story is unique, as no two people have the same experiences; yet, the patterns of the narratives found in them follow an oft-used plot drawn from the place of community. Testimonies tend to describe a struggle building up to a pivotal period when God somehow comes through and renews hope. Faith journeys tend to depict the rhythms of trust and doubt in God in relation to life events and places. Call stories tend to move from sensing that God is addressing us to a period of denial to acceptance: "Here I am, Lord." Such storylines live as resources in the traditions of place through the accumulated witness of the saints and favored stories of scripture. With each telling and retelling of experiences, individuals are *authoring* themselves through the resources of traditions, and in turn these traditions are *author-izing* individuals when personal narratives embody those flowing in the tradition—the authority of tradition is the power given them to author identity and vocation.

To find a story that rings true to our experiences, we need to be aware of the type of story we seek. To understand a text we are reading, it is very important to know whether we are dealing with poetry, mystery, science fiction, history, or religious autobiography. Testimonies of faith and call stories share some themes, but they are different types of stories. Testimonies witness to God's involvement in our lives. Call stories are about vocation and attempt to describe the trajectory and ultimate aim of one's life. In the years after college, I was deeply engaged in a search for such a storyline and was quite uncertain whether the genre of calling was the right one. Today, I frame my experiences in a call story, but with each retelling of those years following college, I continue to re-create meaning—sorting things out once again, getting new insight, redeeming experiences into an evolving sense of direction. Our telling and retelling of life experiences is an *ongoing* process of finding a storyline that provides a sense of identity and purpose.

IDENTITY, VOCATION, AND PLACE

Finding a storyline for identity and purpose in Christian traditions requires facing the questions of *whose* we are and what vocation we claim as ours.[2] The answers to these questions are deeply and profoundly intertwined with place.

The primary theological answer to whose we are is that we belong to God our creator. *We are creatures of God.* An equally important, and theological, answer is that we also belong to *places*—the contexts and relationships in which God's creating call arises. Saying that we belong to place is not some form of romanticized parochialism; rather, it is a way of naming the embodied human, ecological, physical, and spiritual relationships that constitute our identity. God's creative work of forming life from the soil of Eden continues to this day. In each moment of experience, God offers the most redemptive and life-giving way to form our past and the elements gathered by place into relationships that make us who we are. *We are creatures of place.* We can only know our vocations if we see them embedded in places—and making a difference in those places.

God's creative power beckons and redeems rather than coerces and condemns. It is a power of lure and call. This means that creation has freedom to accept or reject, in part or in whole, God's vision for who we are and for relationships. This freedom is often used to explain the capacity for sin and evil in the world. It also explains our capacity for friendship and partnership with God in the world. In the Farewell Discourse in John 15:15, Jesus says, "I do not call you servants [slaves] any longer, because the servant [slave] does not know what the master is doing; but I have called you friends, because I have made known to you everything that I have heard from my Father." Friendship is rooted in freedom, responsiveness, and relationship. Free then, we play a role in God's ongoing creation. Freedom creates the opportunity for partnership with God's work in the world—the opportunity to be in vocation.

Place is not simply the setting in which identity and vocation are expressed, nor is it the backdrop to the divine-human-creation drama. Place is the fabric of the drama itself, the unfolding web of relationships between God, humans, and creation. Place evokes us into identity and partnership with God. Place and vocation are intertwined in a rhythm of form-giving in which place gathers local elements of experience and vocation responds to God's vision for these elements to become life-giving relationships. We are in *vocation*, with purpose, as we respond to and partner with God's continual creating, redeeming, and sustaining work that forms the elements of place into relationships increasingly reflective of God's Kin-dom.[3] In other words, place gathers together a certain set of people, creatures, plants, climate, and physical structures. The relationships between these take particular forms such as a home, workplace, school, or outdoor area. God is active in places leading them toward the Kin-dom.[3] When we encounter God in a place, God calls us to be more than a spouse, co-worker, student, or friend. Our partnership with God compels us to form relationships in place that are redemptive, sustaining, just, and loving.

Our identity is in belonging to God *and* place. Our purpose, grounded in freedom, is partnering with God in the journey toward the Kin-dom in a concrete context. God is continually offering us creatively redemptive storylines in each moment that provide us identity and purpose amidst the relationships in the places we dwell and between which we pilgrim. These storylines are mediated by the Spirit and the accumulated witnesses cradled in sacred texts and traditions.

FAILURE OF VOCATIONAL IMAGINATION: LIMITED AND DISPLACED

Storylines link moments of experience together in the process of sorting out a sense of identity and purpose. Places in which we dwell and between which we move hold many possible storylines for constructing identity and purpose. Traditions within places author and authorize stories of identity and vocation. We also encounter the important role of place in identity and purpose as we consider the questions of whose we are and vocation.

We belong to God *and* place. In and through place we are called forth into identity and partnership with God. Being conscious of the story-formed process giving rise to identity and purpose and how this is embedded in place may not make discernment easier. Discerning the forms of our partnerships with God's work in the world (vocation) and knowing where we dwell and move are rarely easy because they involve deep commitments, complexities, and life implications. Too often, vocational imagination fails because we look for abstract answers for all time, rather than an embedded call for a particular time and place. Clergy, church professionals, and laity alike unintentionally suffer from a failure of vocational imagination—it is not a conspiracy but an accumulated habit of mind.

Vocational imagination, like faith itself, is a way of being in the world. Imagination is about recognizing connections between things in the world and giving relationships meaningful form. "Place" is the way we imagine the web of relationships in particular areas and the relationship between God and the world in those areas. "Vocation" is the way we imagine God's relationship with the world, God's work in the midst of the world, and ways to partner with it. Failed vocational imagination constrains our ability to sense God in our midst and dis-places us from the enfolding Kindom of God. When we dull our vocational imagination, we foster a slumber that interferes with God's ongoing creation of persons, communities, and nature. Think of the woe of those in parables and stories who slumber and do not see God's work about them.[4]

7

Over the years I have read and heard struggles, questions, and fears people have about vocation through faith journey papers, admission essays, new seminarian classes, advising sessions, and conversations in corporate offices and congregations alike. Often comments suggest an assumption about vocation that is displaced and imagination that is too small—and many of these comments I have voiced myself.

COMMENT	ASSUMPTIONS LIMITING VOCATIONAL IMAGINATION
I feel called by God but I cannot see myself in ministry.	Vocation is limited to certain kinds of ministries.
	Ministry is limited to clergy and professionals.
	Vocation limited to the place of church.
I wish I could find my vocation.	Vocation is an object or trait to possess.
I struggle balancing my vocation with family (school, work, self-care, etc.).	Vocation is limited to one place in life.
	Vocation is limited to one form of serving.
I am afraid I have not been following Jesus long enough to have a vocation.	Vocation begins after reaching a point of maturity in discipleship.
I do not feel good enough to be in vocation.	Vocation requires purity, maturity, or confidence.
I do not feel like I have a vocation now that I am parenting/retired.	Vocation is limited to an occupation or one form of serving.
	Vocation is static.
I can't wait to be done with classes so I can get to my vocation.	Vocation is someplace else, somewhere in the future.
I need to find a setting where I can really express my gifts and vocation.	Vocation is based in individual qualities.
	Place is a backdrop to vocation.
I am not sure I am ready or can leave where I am to be in vocation.	Vocation is disconnected from place.

I also hear connections people make between place and vocation, but often in these comments place is merely the setting for times of discernment or the location for expressing vocation. People talk about place in several ways. Summer camps, retreats, service projects, mission trips, and the like are places integral to stirring vocational awareness. Places where deep conversations about faith and vocation happen often hold significance for persons. Individuals hold powerful emotions in relation to settings where groups or communities expressed affirmation, ambivalence, or doubt about their vocational pursuits.

Unfortunately, conversations and exploration of vocation too often are limited to formal educational settings, be they theological or secular. In such settings, place becomes a matter of contextualizing their profession as they participate in field education and internships—a profession as one participates in field education and internships—that is, bringing vocation to a place one acts upon. Perhaps an exception to tendencies of displacing vocation are persons in diaconal ministry, whose charge is bridging the place of church with the place of the world.

Failed vocational imagination has several indicators:

- Vocation is equated with career, profession, or paid employment.

- Vocation is compartmentalized into isolated roles and statuses.

- There is a sense that the roles and responsibilities one has in various places are in competition with each other, especially when vocation is identified with only one of these places.

- Vocation seems to be static and a thing to possess.

- Clergy and laity have false expectations of each other.

- The vocations of persons with disabilities are dismissed.

- The vocations of children, youth, and older adults are disregarded.

- Attention is limited to human need to the exclusion of the rest of creation.

- Persons fail to recognize the intersections of social, ecological, economic, and personal dynamics.

- Vocation is disconnected from place.

Failed vocational imagination hinders the effectiveness of individuals and the church as a whole in fulfilling their mission of partnership with God's creating, redeeming, and sustaining work in the world in several ways. Vocation is not about whether we enter full-time Christian service. It is about how faith lives in the worlds where we live and breathe. Otherwise, we risk making laity passive and stunting discipleship by reducing it to an individualistic spirituality. Rifts between personal and social holiness and between the church and the world are solidified. We reinforce the perception among younger generations and the people who have a passion to make a difference in the world that the church only has old wineskins to offer them. Collaboration between clergy, church professionals, and laity is impaired and the goals of ministry are constrained.

TOWARD MORE EMPOWERING VOCATIONAL IMAGINATION

Understanding vocation and creating communities that foster vocation is an important part of my work as a faculty member with students, whether they are seeking ordination or not. For me, vocation is both a professional agenda and a process in the evolution of my own sense of purpose and identity. This confluence flows out of my struggles with understanding vocation in young adulthood. Many factors feed into the shape of one's vocational trajectory. One is the continual need to return to disrupting experiences and find redemptive meanings for the sake of our own wholeness and as offerings to the wholeness of others—a form of working out my own salvation.

To foster more robust and empowering vocational imagination, we need to reexamine our assumptions about vocation, reexamine our assumptions about place, *and* explore the interplay between them. It seems that when needing to address an issue, the church tends to think first in terms of programming and education. That is often a good thing, and much of my life has involved such efforts in schools and congregations! However, hoping to revitalize vocational imagination through programming and education may be a case of attempting Heifetz's "technical" change (doing what we do better) when "adaptive" change (rethinking the enterprise itself) is needed. The ideas and arguments in the remainder of this book are resources for reflective conversations and practices that map the terrain of vocational imagination in faith communities. Such resources contribute to raising awareness of contextual assumptions and by way of contrast, whether the ideas presented are embraced in part or whole, as ways to understand place and vocation.

My hope is that reexamining and exploring vocation, place, and their interrelatedness will help move individuals and faith communities toward more empowering vocational imagination. Making such a shift will require us to hold many aspects of vocation and place in energizing and creative tension. We must learn to live with the discomforts of such tension.

My hope is that this study will help us proclaim a robust vocational imagination where

- Everyone is called by God in each moment and anyone one can respond in partnership with God, thus being in vocation—clergy and laity, children and adults, employed and unemployed, abled and disabled, babes in Christ and saints. In a similar manner, the same is true of ministry.

- Vocation is dynamic, rebirthed with each moment of response to God as we move within places, between places, and through the stages of our life.

- We can be set apart for partnership with God without being perfect.

- The embodiments of vocation take a variety of forms within daily life and over our lifespan; place is integral to calling in the moment and to the forms vocation takes.

- Place evokes vocation and is a dynamic, interconnected, and inclusive habitat.

- Gifts and graces are birthed in place and become part of our capacities for vocation.

- Vocation arises in individuals and in community at the same time.

- Vocation and place are deeply couched in creation as a whole, not just humans.

11

- Place is a crucial way of engaging the intersectionality of many issues we face as we partner in the unfolding of God's Kin-dom.

In many ways, my hope for renewed vocational imagination is that it calls us to love, identify with, have empathy for, and care for place. I find it meaningful to adopt *topophilia* as a name for such a call. The term combines the Greek *topos* (place) and *philia* (affectionate regard and friendship). Yi-Fu Tuan developed the concept of topophilia in the field of humanistic geography: "The word *topophilia* is a neologism, useful in that it can be defined broadly to include all of the human being's affective ties with the material environment."[5] When I use the term *topophilia*, I take "material environment" in Tuan's definition to be inclusive of human, ecological, cultural, and physical spheres. Tim Cresswell notes,

> The term "topophilia" was developed by Tuan to refer to the "affective bond" between people and place. This bond, this sense of attachment, is fundamental to the idea of place as a "field of care."[6]

Topophilia is part of fulfilling the Great Commandment to love God completely and our neighbors as ourselves, for place gathers all that makes us who we are and all that we are to love. Recognizing YHWH as the ground or place of all being, *Hammaqom* ("The Place") is one of the names the rabbis use for God and we can extend this into a metaphor of God as *I Am—Place*. Topophilia unites the two aspects of the Great Commandment as we lovingly encounter *I Am—Place* within the places of life.

Fostering adaptive change in vocational imagination requires involvement of those responsible for leadership, education, and community formation in congregations. In seminary settings, students need to engage the ways their vocational imaginations have been shaped, are in the process of being shaped, and how they envision participating in the development of vocational imagination in places they dwell. They also need to have a good understanding of formative systems in contexts. In congregational settings, the process requires conversation and shared reflection between persons (ordained, professional, and volunteer) involved in congregational leadership, education, worship, discipleship, and mission—embodied practical theology. Perhaps more important, these persons need to engage in this conversation because of the way implicit actions teach and model vocation. The implicit is very powerful in shaping imagination; social interaction shapes vocational imagination. Those engaged in this project do so to benefit themselves as well as those with whom they minister because the vocational imagination we teach is the one in which we dwell.

LOOKING AHEAD

To develop vocational imagination, we must delve into assumptions about the nature of God's work in the world, the nature of vocation, the nature of place, and the nature of the self. Chapter 2 will frame God's work in the world as forming relationships for flourishing of life and the Spirit—in essence, place-making. This involves considering the gathering of grace, the gathering of brokenness, and the gathering of wholeness. Chapter 3 encourages a rethinking of vocation by first examining several theological themes shaping vocational imagination and then three conceptual tensions in vocation. These tensions are between following and partnering, vocational stability and evolution, and vocation that is personally based and contextually evoked. In brief, vocation will be presented as a process of partnership with God's work in and for the world within particular places. The call to partnership comes from God, but the places we dwell evoke it. Chapter 4 presents an understanding of place from which to engage vocational reflection. More than a location on a map, place is a particular collection of formative relationships rather than merely a location in space—it is the web of relationships from which we come to be and to which we contribute. The central characteristic of place is its power to gather. As with the chapter on vocation, this chapter examines several theological themes shaping our understanding of place. Three particular assumptions are challenged—that places are static, that places are parochial, and that places are anthropocentric. Chapter 5 explores the nature and capacities of the self who is in partnership with God. The capacities for partnership with God include faith, hope, love, integrity, agency, and mutuality. Because the self is constructed by narratives, the robustness of vocation in a faith community is a function of the richness of vocational stories held and valued in that community.

Renewed thinking about vocation and place needs integration with theological praxis. Chapters 6 and 7 address ways of engaging vocation. Chapter 6 attends to the places we dwell and movements in vocationally engaging places. Chapter 7 parallels chapter 6 in attending to the routes we travel and movements in vocationally engaging routes. The main movements for engagement involve naming ways we are connected to a place or a route, identifying who and what are gathered in a place or on a route, recognizing ways a place or a route gathers the self, assessing the nature of relationships in a place or on a route in light of the flourishing of life and the Spirit, and discovering ways of partnering in God's place-making and way-making work. Chapter 8 considers implications for practical theology and for fostering vocation-in-place. In terms of practical theology, place functions as the subject of practical theology (a theology of place) and as an orientation for practical theology itself. I suggest that practical theology may in essence be vocational theology. In terms of equipping persons for vocation-in-place, we need to consider calling into a place of leadership, how we think of congregations as places in themselves, the goals of equipping ministry, and approaches to fostering vocation-in-place.

FOR REFLECTION

Personal Perspective

1. In what ways has your discernment of vocation been easy and difficult? What contributed to either the clarity or difficulty?

2. What role did place have in your discernment process?

3. What commonalities do you recognize in call and vocational stories that you hear from friends and mentors? Is there a difference in stories told by laypersons and clergy? What are the implicit messages about the nature of vocation in such stories? . . . about who does and does not have a calling?

4. Which, if any, of the comments in the table on pages 8–9 do you resonate with and why? What comments from your experience would you add? How do these reflect your assumptions about vocation?

5. How have individuals and faith communities shaped your imagination about vocation? How have you encountered failed vocational imagination and what are the reasons for the failure?

6. For what do you long in your sense of vocation?

Leadership Perspective

7. How do you assist others in their discernment of vocation? What have you observed about what makes such discernment easy or difficult?

8. How do you see persons connecting their vocation with a sense of place?

9. How do you tell your story of assuming ordained, professional, or lay leadership to others? What does the way you tell this story implicitly teach about vocation and calling?

10. What are ways that you expand and limit other's vocational imagination?

11. What are your hopes for the vocations of those you lead?

Congregational Perspective

12. In what ways does your faith community have clarity and difficulties in discerning its collective vocation?

13. What role does place play in the vocation of the congregation?

14. What seems to be the collective vocation of the congregation?

15. How does the congregation foster and hinder vocational imagination?

from many places. In turning the tables, I think Mom was partnering with God in place-making and shaping my vocational imagination.

THE GATHERING WORK OF GOD

A central feature of place is its power to gather and, as *I Am—Place*, God gathers the world into being. However, in what *kind* of gathering is God engaged?

A range of answers to that question exists within Christian traditions, and they shape our vocational imagination. The Great Commission (Matt 28:18-20) points to God reconciling the world to God and forming disciples. When Jesus invokes the Jewish Shema[1] in Matthew 22:35-39, many Christians think of Jesus as proclaiming the "Great Commandment" that deeply links love of God with love of others and emphasizes how God fosters in us love for neighbors. The formation of Israel told in the Hebrew Bible and development of the body of Christ depicted in the New Testament reveal God's attention to fostering new communal ways of being human together.[2] The expectations of Micah 6:8—"He has told you, O mortal, what is good; and what does the Lord require of you but to do justice, and to love kindness, and to walk humbly with your God"—emphasize God's work to create a world of peaceable and just relationships. The parable of the final judgment scene in Matthew 25, where those who inherit the realm of God are the ones who cared for the least, reflects God's care for the suffering and marginalized in the world. Trinitarian doctrines highlight God's communal nature and God's creating, saving, and sustaining work. Christocentric theologies stress God working to save the world from sin and brokenness and to bring fullness (flourishing) of life. You likely can add many other answers to this list.

I think a thread running through the above responses to what God is doing in the world is that God is fashioning relationships that are creative, freeing, just, and faithful—relationships in which life and the Spirit flourish. This is gathering work—forming relationships in the places we dwell and the routes we travel in light of the Kin-dom of God. As we form relationships, we do so with reverence for ways the Kin-dom is already

19

present, with ire for the ways the Kin-dom is in travail, and with hope for the fullness of the Kin-dom yet to come.

Human, ecological, and spiritual flourishing requires many things. In the healings of Jesus, we consistently see return to wholeness as involving physical well-being, spiritual rebirth, and by restoration to community. Flourishing emerges through positive and generative relationships. In the United States, individualism often causes persons to overlook this dynamic because it assumes that independence of individuals is more fundamental than their relationships. This is evident religiously when congregations only emphasize God's concern for the individual. For example, a common reading of the parable of the lost sheep (Luke 15:1-7) focuses on the love of the shepherd for each individual sheep. However, this parable also reflects the brokenness of the flock in light of the lost sheep's absence. We should not lose sight of how the return of the lost sheep makes the flock whole. What constitutes flourishing reflects a millennia-old debate in philosophy and religion about what constitutes the good life—and this debate is fraught with projecting a perceived universal "good" onto others. In some ways, describing what hinders flourishing, the ways of death, is easier than naming what flourishing entails.[3]

Therefore, the task of partnership with God's work in the world is about forming relationships that foster flourishing of life and the Spirit. The relationships between what places and routes gather may or may not reflect such flourishing. In fact, the relationships in place may do just the opposite—they may foster death of life and the Spirit. This runs counter to the gathering work of God, who calls us into creative, redemptive, just, and loving relationships. Our partnership in this gathering work of God requires discerning the dynamics that produce both deadening and flourishing of life and the Spirit in places and on routes. In other words, awareness of sin and grace in place. I use these power-full words with caution.

Grace and sin are categories of values connected to assumptions about what is good and what is evil. When coupled with the dynamics of power that shape a given place, privileged groups may use sin and grace in destructive and divisive ways. Privilege sets norms in favor of some at the expense of others and does so in relation to places, whether one seeks this privilege or not. The structures of privilege in the bar next to a foundry are not the same as those in a gastropub. The privileges in a suburban congregation are not the same as those in an urban one. Privilege uses "sin" as a way to define what does not belong in a place—what is out of place and mis-placed. Rather than seeking the Kin-dom of relationships, we fall into habits of purging and defining as sinful anything we perceive as not belonging. In a similar manner, privilege uses "grace" as a way to name characteristics of the in-group as virtues and unique blessing of their place. In comparison, other peoples and places are deficient.

My caution in using the language of sin is a matter of taking seriously the hazards of self-deception rather than wanting to be nice or inoffensive. The language of sin is easily corrupted by conflating my judgments with that of God. When I do this, my personal, social, cultural, and ecological prejudices and privilege seem God-ordained, which leads to denigration, dis-placement, and suffering of others. Labeling things as sin becomes sin-full in itself. As one receiving many types of privilege from my social location, I am particularly susceptible to this and must be vigilant against it. At the same time, by not naming situations of human, ecological, and spiritual suffering as sin, I may come to accept such brokenness fatalistically as the way of the world, which may lead to passivity. Not naming brokenness as sin becomes sin-full complicity in suffering.

In light of these concerns and risks, why even use the language of sin and grace? Some communities within and related to Christian traditions avoid such language. I retain these terms because we cannot escape the moral challenges at the intersection of values and power. Discernment is difficult religious and ethical work. Additionally, while in contexts of privilege the language of sin and grace can be used oppressively, they can support liberative work in non-privileged settings. In such settings, naming systemic sin is an act of resistance and claiming graces an act of empowerment and resiliency.[4]

If God is working in the world for the flourishing of life and the Spirit, then what deadens is at odds with this work and being at cross-purposes with God is one description of sin. I wish to be clear that this discussion *is about the assessment and consequences of actions on relationships*

and flourishing for the purposes of discerning partnership with God in place.
I am *not* addressing the question of whether human nature is inherently
sinful. Neither am I embracing the "hate the sin, love the sinner" mental-
ity. Brokenness and suffering are concrete indicators of gathering that is
contrary to God's intentions and easier to recognize than abstract prohibi-
tions. Judgments about the moral and salvific status of people I leave to
God. So, how might we consider the ways places gather their members
into relationships and flourishing?

GATHERING GRACE, BROKENNESS, AND WHOLENESS

Places gather the attitudes, assumptions, emotions, and expectations
of those in a place. These come together to form a perspective about a
place that influences the ability to recognize assets for flourishing, brokenness that deadens, and feelings of hope and despair. Biases about a place
can lead to monolithic perspectives about it—seeing a place only in terms
of its brokenness, needs, and deficiencies. A congregation, even with nothing but good intentions, may become so focused on helping a "needy"
neighborhood (its own or another) that it cannot see that neighborhood
as anything but deficient and dependent. The assets for flourishing become invisible. Conversely, biases can lead one to see a place only in terms
of its prosperity, assets, and strengths. A suburban congregation may become so accustomed to the perceived successfulness of its neighborhood
that it is unaware of homelessness, hunger, and violence in its midst.

For the purposes of discerning partnership with God, we need to consider ways places gather both assets and needs, hope and despair, grace
and brokenness. God is at work blessing gifts and repairing brokenness—
so should our partnership with God. If we do not attend to the giftedness of place, partnership becomes primarily problem-solving and fixing
the situations of others. Certainly, there is plenty in the world to repair.
However, attending to giftedness provides resources for resiliency to face
brokenness, for the work of repair, and more important for creating new
ways of being whole. Grace and assets in one's view of place and routes

shifts dependency to mutuality, pity to solidarity, giving to stewardship, problem-solving to flourishing. We should more often begin our discernment of partnership in place with questions of assets and graces.

Engaging both the grace and brokenness of place and ourselves also shapes our connection with place. It provides honesty needed for liberative relationships. It provides a basis for recognizing our shared circumstances that supports respect and empathy with each other.

Gathering Grace

For the purposes of discerning partnership with God, we need to consider ways places gather grace. We should be careful not to limit our understandings of grace to merely being *freedom from*. The gift of grace liberates us from our habituation to choices that break our personhood and our relationships with others—especially things from which we cannot be liberated by ourselves. However, too often people turn grace into freedom from responsibility. Grace becomes a tool in self-deception, but self-deception is no grace. I have seen this in myself and in classroom conversations about race when white participants are more concerned about being seen as good people and feeling good about themselves than facing their racial biases and actions. Grace is not just freedom from. It is also *freedom for* responsiveness to God, neighbor, and creation. Grace frees us for responsiveness in two ways. First, grace removes impediments to responsiveness. Second, grace empowers by providing gifts and talents that expand our abilities to be responsive to God, neighbor, and creation. We need empowering grace as well as liberating grace. We also depend on the creative life-giving grace woven into the fabric of the universe.[5] This grace is the freedom and resources needed for life. Generative, liberating, and empowering grace contribute to places where relationships and partnership flourish, where life and the Spirit flourish.

There are many ways gathering can reflect generative, liberating, and empowering grace:

- Stewardship that cares for the gifts of place and making gifts accessible for the common good

- Habitats creating a web of resources making life and flourishing possible

23

- Collective advocacy for freedom and justice

- Corporate worship that evokes gratitude

- Gathering the diversity of the body of Christ

- Building community anew with the welcoming of each stranger

- In service, people giving themselves for others

- Education that nurtures and affirms gifts

Gathering Brokenness

For the purposes of discerning partnership with God, we need to consider ways places gather brokenness and, in some cases, death. Two aspects significantly influence how one attends to brokenness gathered by place. One aspect is a tension between the emphases placed on personal and systemic dynamics. A second aspect is the interrelatedness of differing forms of brokenness.

The tension between personal and social dynamics has roots in how one locates the source of sin. Some see sin as a result of personal choices, and others see sin coming from broken human systems. Naturally, this shapes whether one works to advance flourishing by focusing on the transformation of individuals or social systems. Flourishing of life and the Spirit requires overcoming this false personal and social dichotomy. The absence of good socio-ecological relationships hinders flourishing and having good socio-ecological relationships without some level of individual wholeness and grace is a challenge.

Brokenness and suffering in place do not arise from single sources. They arise from the weaving together of personal, social, ecological, and spiritual dimensions of life. Also, within these dimensions, systems such as racism, sexism, classism, ableism, heterosexism, and anthropocentrism shape experience individually and in conjunction with each other. Even when we are conscious of particular systemic issues in place, we can be oblivious to the ways they work in combination with each other. Recognizing the interplay of systems is one of the benefits of utilizing a place framework. It allows for—indeed demands—attention to the interaction of systems.

Intersectionality

Intersectionality is a way of describing the interplay of hierarchies of power and privilege at work in the relational fabric of place. Used in conjunction with place, intersectionality "investigates how individuals and groups get placed, place themselves and also place others, both physically, structurally and rhetorically."[6] Intersectionality helps us move beyond simple interrelatedness to addressing ways the interaction of such social systems empower and hinder wholeness. Intersectionality

> posits that socially constructed categories of oppression and privilege, such as race, class, gender, and age, simultaneously interact to create unique life experiences.... Women of color argued strongly that race, class, and gender are inseparable determinates of inequalities that interdependently "form interlocking patterns. The interlocking patterns in turn serve as bases for developing multiple systems of domination that affect access to power and privileges, influence social relationships, construct meanings, and shape people's everyday experience."[7]

In reviewing literature on intersectionality, Mike Parent, Cirleen DeBlaere, and Bonnie Moradi note that understandings of intersectionality "share as a common thread the recognition of multiple interlocking identities that are defined in terms of relative sociocultural power and privilege and shape people's individual and collective identities and experiences."[8] The intersectionality framework engages dynamics within particular systems, as well as the interplay between those systems.

To utilize intersectionality fully as a framework for shaping vocational imagination, we need to include the created world and environmental issues as part of the patterns of experience and power. Intersectionality needs to be ecological literacy as well as social literacy.[9] Environmental oppression intersects with race and class as one considers the location of hazardous industries, pollution concentrations, and food deserts. Access to environmental assets, such as green spaces and quality food, is as important to consider, as are environmental liabilities.

Intersectionality is a powerful construct for understanding the dynamics of injustice and oppression. This is true not only for those experiencing injustice but also for those experiencing privilege. For example, intersectionality brings attention to co-constituting dimensions of race and gender that are oppressive for a woman of color while privileging for a white man. Additionally, intersectionality notes the fluidity of oppression and privilege. A woman of color and a white woman are both subject to sexism, but in terms of racism the white woman receives privilege. Places are social and environmental topographies across which the fluidity of intersectionality (and hybridity) that one experiences and embodies flows. *Place shapes where, when, and how one experiences injustice and privilege.*

With the aid of an intersectionality perspective, we can recognize many ways gathering can embody brokenness and suffering:

- Colonialism oppressively gathers peoples, their resources, and their land for the use of others.

- Mass incarceration goes beyond public safety to gather marginalized peoples into prisons.

- Segregation gathers people deemed different into stigmatized, controlled, and suppressed places.

- Genocide gathers people into concentration camps and killing fields.

- Abuse gathers people in households of privatized violence.

- Market changes gather persons into communities of impoverishment and despair.

- Addictions gather personal choices into patterns of dependency.

- Violence and desperation gather people into places of exile.

- Gentrification gathers areas from low-income and marginally housed persons.

- Development gathers land from natural habitats.

- Traditionalism gathers people into rigid pasts.

Vocational Imagination within Brokenness

Failure of vocational imagination is often the result of limited models and understandings of vocation. Brokenness influences vocational imagination as well, by interfering with place's ability to evoke us into vocation. *Privilege* creates a sense of obliviousness to and independence from place. *Enmeshment* in place creates a sense of fatalism and closure. *Displacement* creates a sense of alienation and exile. *Anthropocentrism* creates a sense of self-sufficiency. *Injustice* creates barriers and a sense of disempowerment.[10]

Privilege fractures vocational imagination by creating a sense that place has no (or relatively little) effect on you. One is oblivious to place.[11] Functionally, others (human and nonhuman) become invisible and voiceless to those benefiting from privilege. This situation disrupts the vocation of both those privileged and those made invisible, voiceless, and deprived of worth unto themselves. When I am the recipient of privilege—and I live at the epicenter of many privileges—I can move through and function in places without adapting who I am. I presume an independence from the relationships of place because those relationships lack the power to exercise claims on me.

Enmeshment in place fractures vocational imagination by making it seem you have no (or relatively little) effect on place—place becomes something that just "is." As privilege can make others invisible, being enmeshed in a place can make that place invisible or a mere backdrop to human activity. Enmeshment disrupts vocational imagination in at least two ways. First, *we become fatalistic* and cannot imagine how our place(s) can change, at least for the better. Fatalism robs place of the power to evoke vocation because place becomes lifeless. Second, *we enclose place in a myopic way* and cannot imagine how our place(s) are not normative (i.e., the way all places should be). Myopic place becomes a strand in an ideological cocoon,[12] a type of common sense that suppresses consciousness of place and thus its power to evoke. Fatalism and myopia undercut the ability of place to evoke vocation and our agency to respond to place in vocation.

Displacement fractures vocational imagination by distancing or removing us from place. We neither feel like we belong to nor have a place—one has a persistent sense of alienation and exile. Displacement can be physical, social, psychological, and ecological. It can be the result of being a refugee from violence, oppression, victimization, or trafficking; exile from origins; social alienation; personal and family estrangement; being cut off from nature; and social mobility. In an age where the self is increasingly hybrid (i.e., identity is increasingly "hyphenated"), many persons are unsure of where they belong. The sense of not belonging makes it difficult to have enough affinity with any place to enable it to evoke vocation. Fear and vulnerability may impede responsiveness to vocation as well—is there enough connection with place to risk engaging in vocation there?

Anthropocentrism is the belief that humanity is the central focus of creation and that whatever is nonhuman derives its value based on its contributions to humanity. It is a form of privilege, one based on valuing humans over the rest of creation. I am treating anthropocentrism separately from other forms of privilege because of the scope of its effect. Other forms of privilege obviously affect very large groups of people, but anthropocentrism hides most of creation from the vocational horizon. Anthropocentrism makes creation, a vital part of place, either silent or subservient to wishes of human and thus loses its role in evoking vocation. Anthropocentrism creates a sense of human self-sufficiency and independence from creation. It also contributes to other forms of privilege and injustice, because one way we can deem others as misplaced and disposable is to view them as nonhuman—to make them like the rest of nature. Anthropocentrism severely limits the scope of what evokes us into vocation. We cannot value what we do not recognize.

Injustice actively creates barriers to connecting with place, with others, and with vocation, as well as undercutting the agency of persons to act. Here I am thinking in terms such as racism, sexism, classism, ableism, heterosexism, and colonialism. Injustice does violence to places and those that dwell in them. Those who suffer such harm are resilient—they connect to place, value their relationships, know their giftedness, and are evoked to vocation. However, contravening powers and principalities persist against them through explicit and implicit, physical and psychological, violent and coercive means. Injustice is a frontal assault on vocational imagination and place.

The influence of intersectionality on vocational imagination is not all negative. Places of intersection, and even margins, provide powerful insights. One of the benefits of viewing vocation in relation to place is precisely the power of place to gather—to be an embodiment of intersectionality. Creativity, critical awareness, and energy are at the intersection that is "place"—and thus place itself becomes the precise location that evokes us most powerfully into vocation and to respond most faithfully in *place-making*.[13]

Gathering Wholeness

For the purposes of discerning partnership with God, we need to consider ways places gather wholeness in the presence of both grace and brokenness. By this, I mean ways life and the Spirit can flourish even if in constrained ways within the messy mix of assets and needs, blessings and brokenness, joy and pain in a place. While partnering with God to help redeem brokenness, we should be aware that redemption alone is not sufficient for flourishing. Even if we could entirely redeem and eliminate brokenness, one may not flourish. Joy is not the absence of pain. Love is not merely the absence of hate. Life is not the merely absence of death. Brokenness is not the first nature of things—grace is. Wholeness more importantly involves gathering grace. Gathering grace in the midst of brokenness means deepening awareness of resources, drawing together what resources are present, leveraging such resources, and using them for wholeness. Gathered grace leads to resiliency, agency, adaptability, creativity—freedom from circumstances being determinative of one's wholeness.[14]

FORMING RELATIONSHIPS— PLACE-MAKING

Place-making is partnering in God's ongoing creation of right relationships and flourishing of life. As noted earlier, there are several ways to understand God's intentions for relationships and flourishing. My inclination to interpret things in terms of the Kin-dom of God is probably apparent by now. Place-making takes these broad understandings of God's intentions and makes them concrete in the localness of place. Place-making is a way to understand the interaction between vocation and place.[15]

We are always giving form to relationships, resources, and power as part of the normal course of experience, whether we are conscious of it or not. We are place-making faithfully when we foster community, practice hospitality and mutuality, steward the environment, deepen spirituality, manifest the divine in our bodies and physical spaces, heal brokenness, nurture growth, and pursue peace with justice.

Place-making is an expression of topophilia, redemption, and wholeness. Topophilia is the love of and solidarity with a particular gathering of human and ecological relationships. Redemption is the constant process of valuing and revaluing the relationships and experiences that contribute to who we are becoming. This broadens the idea of redemption from just finding something meaningful in brokenness (healing) to living into the graces of life (flourishing).

To speak of place-making runs the risk of becoming anthropocentric—a risk we must intentionally and reflectively avoid. Our agency in place-making does not mean we are the sole agents of place-making. All that place gathers is participating in place-making—human and non-human. We also risk self-deception about our interests and motivations when we see place-making as something we do on behalf of others. Place-making is not a value neutral endeavor, nor is it easy.

SUMMARY

Understandings about God's relationship with the world and about God's work in the world are essential to vocational reflection. The diversity of such understandings within Christianity makes it a tradition of traditions—a centuries-old conversation about God's purposes and about what we are called to be in relation to those purposes. Such tradition-producing conversations do more than generate theological doctrines. They foster a vision for the purposes of faith and life—they foster a vocational imagination. By centering on the work of God that gathers the world into being and that forms relationships that provide fullness of life and the Spirit, I wish to name a shared thread for vocational conversations rather than obscure the breadth of Christian tradition.

By their nature, places and routes gather as well. In that process, they gather grace and they gather brokenness. The extent to which places and routes gather redemptive wholeness depends a great deal on our responsiveness to the call of God in and through places. This ongoing call is to partnership in creating relationships from what is gathered in places and on routes that foster fullness of life and the Spirit. We partner with God in gathering graces, redeeming brokenness, and finding wholeness reflective of the Kin-dom of God—we partner in the work of place-making. The particular and unique nature of that work depends on where we are and who we are. In the next chapter, we will begin rethinking assumptions about vocation to better understand the particularities of our partnership with God.

FOR REFLECTION

Personal Perspective

1. What are places in your life that significantly shaped your understanding of relationships between people, and between people and the rest of creation?

2. What do you think God is seeking to do in the world?

3. What do you think is needed for the flourishing of life and the Spirit... generally and in the places you dwell?

4. How do you define sin and how does that understanding relate to the places you live and the routes you travel?

5. How do you define grace and how does that understanding relate to the places you live and the routes you travel?

6. How do forces creating injustice and privilege intersect in the places you dwell and the routes you travel? How do they shape where, when, and how one experiences injustice and privilege?

7. What are ways that the brokenness of place has hindered your sense of vocation?

8. What are ways that the graces of place have fostered your sense of vocation?

9. Describe ways that you are partnering with God in gathering graces, redeeming brokenness, and finding wholeness reflective of the Kin-dom of God—place-making.

Leadership Role Perspective

10. What are you implicitly teaching about the nature of relationships between people and between people, and the rest of creation through the ways you gather persons for meetings, worship, learning, service, and meals?

11. What are you explicitly and implicitly teaching about the following:

    a. What God is seeking to do in the world?

    b. Sin and grace in the places and routes of life?

    c. How forms of brokenness intersect with each other?

12. In what ways are you removing obstacles to and amplifying assets for individual and collective vocation?

13. How are you equipping persons for partnering with God in gathering graces, redeeming brokenness, and finding wholeness reflective of the Kin-dom of God—place-making?

Congregational Perspective

14. What does the congregation implicitly teach about the nature of relationships between people, and between people and the

rest of creation through the ways it gather persons for meetings, worship, learning, service, and meals?

15. What seems to be the assumptions in the congregation about the following:

    a. What God is seeking to do in the world?

    b. Sin and grace in the places and routes of life?

    c. How forms of brokenness intersect with each other?

16. What obstacles to and assets for vocation are present in the congregation?

17. Name some examples of ways persons are gathering graces, redeeming brokenness, and finding wholeness reflective of the Kin-dom of God—place-making.

Chapter 3

PARTNERSHIP WITH GOD IN PLACE: RETHINKING VOCATION

A DAY IN THE LAB

One day I was in the engineering lab at work and I wandered over to Rusty's technician bench. Even though Rusty was not working on one of my projects, we had developed a good connection. It was a class day for me, which meant hustling off to the seminary from the office and, as soon as class was finished, dashing back to the office. Jumping from place to place was not just a physical trick—it took existential agility as well and often left me wondering what I was getting myself into by taking seminary classes.

Rusty knew I was taking classes and I said something about the existential gymnastics and my discernment muddle. There was a pause and then he started sharing part of his story, which left me very unsettled. Not long after becoming Christian, Rusty felt a calling to ministry, by which he meant pastoral ministry. He eventually quit his job and moved his family to Anderson in order to attend the same seminary as I was attending. During the course of his studies, he became certain that being a pastor was not his calling. He'd worked as a technician at General Motors since that time and was an active member of a congregation as a layperson. Rusty told his story somberly. He did not sound bitter or regretful, but neither did it sound like one of those everything-works-out-in-the-end stories. There was a bit of silence at the end of his story. I tried to offer appreciation for what he shared and words of encouragement. Those words were hard to find in light of my own discernment dilemma. The shared awkwardness ended as we returned to our respective work.

Rusty's story stuck with me. While I had not uprooted my family, I was potentially putting many things on the line by taking seminary classes—home life, career, finances. Regardless of whether I remained an engineer or became a pastor, what if I was sadly mistaken about my calling like Rusty? Focusing solely on these questions reduced the issues of vocation to one of discernment. Questions about the nature of vocation itself would have helped me even more.

Understandings about God's work in the world greatly influence vocational imagination. So too do our assumptions about the nature of vocation itself, and this chapter explores those assumptions. The starting point will be reflection on several theological themes, such as human nature, that do not explicitly address vocation but nonetheless influence vocational assumptions. Next, we will consider three neglected aspects of vocation that make important contributions to rethinking the nature of vocation—vocation is active partnership with God, vocation is a process, and vocation is evoked by place. After addressing assumptions that influence understandings of vocation, I will present a definition of vocation as a *process of partnership* with God's work in and for the world within and *evoked by particular places*.

In the lab with Rusty, I assumed vocation was a thing to find—a role out there somewhere. Not finding it was to be outside God's will for me. I wonder what would have happened if I had understood that vocation is not a thing to possess but a process that has everything to do with where you are and where you go. As for Rusty, he may not have become a pastor, but he was partnering with God in the place of that lab . . . and all the other places of his life.

APPROACHING VOCATION THEOLOGICALLY

Reflective, respectful, and candid conversations about vocation are essential for the formation of vibrant vocational imagination—and for the vitality of historical traditions as a whole. Alasdair MacIntyre suggests that tradition is a community having a conversation about its core stories, beliefs, values, and practices. When deep conversation stops, imagination and the traditions that inspire them die. Imagination withers to repetition and, paraphrasing Jaroslav Pelikan, tradition as the living faith of the dead becomes traditionalism's dead faith of the living.[1] Such conversations identify assumptions, habits of mind, and practices to create a mosaic of a shared reality—constructing a shared place.

Vocation, within the places called faith communities, is profoundly shaped by church traditions and theological dispositions within them. Not all communities of faith, or even public communities, use the language of vocation. The influence of Rick Warren's *The Purpose Driven Life* points to a longing in many Christians to make an intentional difference in the world and reflects vocation framed as Christian purpose. Frederick Buechner's description of vocation from *Theological ABCs* as the intersection of our deepest longings and the world's greatest needs is often cited. Parker Palmer in *Let Your Life Speak* frames vocation as grounded in the authentic self. Vocational themes may find expression in terms such as the priesthood of all believers, spiritual giftedness, doing the will of God, doing all things to the glory of God, Christian service, responsiveness to need, fulfilling a job, serving as an effective volunteer, or living into an authentic self who is true to what God wishes of us.

Our conversations need to work with the theological assumptions and dynamic tensions at play in vocational imagination. We can think of theological doctrines as responses to essential questions of a faith community informing belief, attitudes, and practices. Given the scope, complexity, and significance of such questions, theological doctrines typically embody tensions in their response. For example, responses to questions about the nature of Christ embody tensions between Jesus being fully human and fully divine. *As we consider the interplay between specific theological doctrines and our vocational imagination, we must engage inherent theological tensions.*

Tensions, as used here, are creative and meaningful dynamics rather than inherently problematic forces needing resolution. We have a tendency in the church to reduce such tensions into dichotomies. Problems arise when tensions collapse and their invigorating energies are lost. Imagine a suspension bridge that depends on the tensions in its varied cables and struts to maintain its integrity and fulfill its purpose. Should tensions be relieved (or destructively overdone) the bridge fails. Meaningful theology and vocational imagination suffer when we neglect or lose sight of components that contribute to life-giving tensions. Imagination enables us to creatively engage in both/and thinking.

We must also engage a range of theological doctrines because no single doctrine answers all questions of faith. Responding to questions of vocation means drawing upon doctrines of human nature, transformation, God and world, revelation, Trinity, church mission, and church. Each of these doctrines deserves extensive treatment and much more nuance, but I invite you to consider these prompts for exploring connections between theology and vocational imagination.

Human Nature

One theological tension is between humanity being basically good but prone to error and humanity being essentially corrupted and embedded in sin. This tension influences the degree to which one trusts in human agency to discern faithfully and carry out God's will. Another theological tension is between humans as communal (persons-in-community) and as independent individuals. As creatures made in the image of a trinitarian God, this suggests that our nature is communal and interrelated with others. Vocationally, this shapes the degree to which one views vocational discernment as a communal process and vocational efforts as shared with others. Forms of a social-personal tension exist in several theological themes. This illustrates the interplay between doctrinal assumptions and the need to consider them collectively. *Our vocational imagination needs to embrace human giftedness and human brokenness so we have honest hope about making a faithful difference where we dwell.*

Transformation

A theological tension here is between redemptive transformation initiated on the social level and that pursued by changing one individual soul at a time. The vocational connection rests in how one focuses vocation on social-individual dimensions. A second tension is the role of the Holy Spirit and human effort in redemptive transformation. Similarly to questions of human nature, the vocational concern is the extent of human agency in shaping the places we dwell. *Our vocational imagination needs prophetically to engage personal and social holiness where we dwell.*

God and World

This theological theme focuses on God's relationship to the world and the tension we find is between God's immanence (presence in the material world) and God's transcendence (differentiation from the world). The more one emphasizes immanence and incarnation, the more likely partnership with God in place shapes vocational imagination. The more one emphasizes transcendence, the more likely vocational imagination can become bringing God to a godless place. *Our vocational imagination needs to trust God's presence in places we dwell and trust in God's greater movement.*

Revelation

When thinking of revelation, often scripture (special revelation) comes to mind but it also includes God's self-disclosure in creation and world (general revelation). The tension between once-and-for-all revelation (static) and ongoing revelation (dynamic) intertwines with that of special and general revelation. Questions of revelation connect to those of the relationship between God and world. These tensions influence how we discern God's call and will for living in place and the degree to which we see vocation as evolving. *Our vocational imagination needs formation by the combined witnesses of scripture and tradition and by openness to the One who makes all things new where we dwell.*

Trinity

The Trinity is an enigma, doctrine, and mystery where a trilateral tension involves the persons of the Trinity. Our theological imagination tends to gravitate toward one person in the Trinity, which has vocational implications. The *ontological* expression of the Trinity is Father-Son-Holy Spirit and reflects the inner relationships of the three. The ontological Trinity shapes our imagination of the Person with whom we are in vocational partnership. The *economic* expression of the Trinity is Creator-Redeemer-Sustainer and reflects God's work in the world. This Trinity shapes our imagination about the nature of the work in place in which we partner. *Our vocational imagination needs diverse ways to encounter God as guide to our vocation and diverse ways to recognize God's involvement in the world.*

Church

At least two tensions, if not more, exist in how we conceive of the church. One, dealing with the nature of the church, is between the church as the body of Christ and the church as a human institution. This dynamic shapes how we see our vocation as interwoven with those of others and the degree of trust we place in others to guide and empower vocation. A second tension exists when dealing with the structure of the church, and whether leadership is hierarchical or egalitarian. This structural tension influences our vocational imagination in terms of how we are accountable to others and how we understand the roles of ordained, professional, and lay ministry (indeed, whether or not everyone has a vocation). *Our vocational imagination needs to draw upon the discerning wisdom and empowering support of others for vocations that are faithful and sustained.*

Church Mission

Perhaps a key tension in the mission of the church is between the Great Commission to make disciples (Matt 28:16-20) and the Great Commandment to love God and neighbor (Matt 22:36-40). Although both involve teaching and developing relationship with God, some draw upon the Great Commission to emphasize evangelization and others draw upon the Great Commandment to emphasize service to others and social engagement. This tension shapes how we imagine the purpose of our vocation in place. *Our vocational imagination needs to connect deep discipleship with expressions of respectful witness and compassionate service in places we dwell.*

Theological Connections with Vocational Imagination

Theological Theme	Theological Tension			Vocational Issue
Human Nature	Good but often misses the mark	⇔	Corrupted and embedded in sin	Trust in human agency to faithfully discern & act
	Communal	⇔	Individual	Mutuality in discernment Shared vocation
Transformation	Social level	⇔	Individual level	Focal arena of vocation
	Holy Spirit	⇔	Human effort	Role of human agency
God and World	Immanence	⇔	Transcendence	Nature of partnership Role of place in vocation
Revelation	General	⇔	Special	Discerning God's will & actions
	Ongoing	⇔	One-time	Evolution of vocation
Trinity	God—Jesus—Spirit			View of person(s) with whom we partner
	Creator—Redeemer—Sustainer			Nature of the work in which we partner
Church Mission	Great Commandment	⇔	Great Commission	Purpose of vocation

Theological Theme	Theological Tension		Vocational Issue
Church	Body of Christ	⇔ Human Institution	View of mutual vocation, shared action, & empowerment
	Hierarchical	⇔ Open-Egalitarian	Understanding of accountability, ordained-professional-lay roles

Before moving on from theological considerations, we should address sin in its systemic institutional form. Such sin dehumanizes persons and subjugates creation to human pleasure. We participate in systems denying that persons are made in the image of God and bear the face of Christ. One of the ways we do this is to impede the freedom of persons to become what God has called them to be. This is sin on two levels as it does harm to others (*sins—particular acts of wrong*) and it opposes God's will (*sin—a state of opposition to and alienation from God*) for that person. Not all closing of vocational options in shared discernment reflect systemic sin—we err as we see through lenses dimly and some options are truly bad for us. However, we do need to address ways systemic sin distorts vocational imagination of various groups—how we see the gifts and graces of others and how people experience the explicit and implicit messages about what one can become. The ways in which the role of laity is understood, how the "spiritual but not religious" are welcomed (or not), and how the privileged majority view less privileged groups all contribute to the way in which vocational possibilities are made available and how the vocational imaginations of the individuals are shaped.

VOCATIONAL TENSIONS

As we considered theological assumptions relative to vocation, we noted tensions shaping vocational imagination. To revitalize vocational

43

imagination, we also need to consider several tensions woven into the concept of vocation itself. I wish to focus on three major tensions in vocation (some having tensions within them as well) and respective neglected aspects that diminish vocational imagination.

Following in Discipleship ←→ Partnering in Vocation

In its fullest embodiment, discipleship involves serving others, and one could rightly argue that vocation is encompassed by true discipleship. Unfortunately, discipleship is too frequently embraced as individualistic spirituality and is framed primarily as followership. Such a framing in the United States context is fostered by several dynamics:

- Individualism in US Christianity shapes discipleship into a personal and inward spiritual journey.

- Within such individualism, service is framed as an *expression* of spirituality and discipleship.

- As an expression of spirituality, expectations to serve may become contingent on reaching certain levels of faith development.

- Within the pervasive clergy paradigm and professional model, discipleship is implicitly cast as followership of congregational leaders with varying degrees of lay passivity.

When discipleship is not held in tension with the core concept of partnership found in vocation, we err on the side of passivity rather than initiative in lived faith. When partnership is not held in tension with following the way of Jesus, we err on the side of assuming our actions are God's will.

Perhaps the tension of following and partnering is connected with two underlying tensions. One holds human nature as deeply flawed *and* as reflecting the image of God. Emphasizing depravity might predispose one to following, while emphasizing the image of God predisposes one to partnering. A second holds spiritual maturity as purity *and* as holiness. Emphasizing purity predisposes to following a sinless Christ; holiness to partnering with an engaged Jesus. Too often purity and holiness are confused. Purity has to do with the absence of what does not belong. Holiness has to do with being set apart for a purpose. Holy water is not holy because it is pure distilled deionized H_2O, but because it has been blessed for sacred use. When the confusion between purity and holiness occurs, holiness is distorted into a bulimic faith obsessed with control and purging whatever is deemed out of place.

Sanctification can be a way of productively holding together the tension of following and partnering. In sanctification we have the dynamics of freedom from the intention and desire to sin and freedom for deepening consistency to say yes in the moment to God's lure of partnership (i.e., vocation). The process of sanctification aligns our desires with the desires of God, leading to God being able to call us friends rather than slaves because we know what the master is about[2]—God has faith in us to choose our heart's desires. The trajectory of vocation over time reflects sanctification.

Vocational Stability ←→ *Vocational Evolution*

The problems of understanding faith as a noun is a common topic in faith development theory. As a noun, faith easily becomes an object of belief, something to hold, rather than a way of being in the world (John Westerhoff)[3] and a process of meaning-making (James Fowler).[4] Vocation suffers from a similar objectification into a static noun—a misplaced concreteness that makes vocation a static thing to possess. Think of the ways we refer to vocation as something one "has" and one "seeks to find."

The claim that objectification of vocation is a mistake is rooted in the assumption that the world is in a continuous process of becoming moment by moment. We arise in a moment; the moment ends and we arise again in the next moment. In each moment of experience, we sense our past and that of the world about us both *human and nonhuman*. God participates in each moment of experience of each part of the world, offering, luring, propositioning, and *calling*, with a way to weave together our past and our radical relationships. That proposition from God offers the most redemptive and life-giving option for us individually and the world as a whole in the moment. God's offering is not coercive—there is radical freedom in each moment to reject in whole or part the proposition from God. Despite such radical freedom, the reality is that the weight of past experience and decisions creates a tendency to replicate prior ways

45

of being and responding to God. In working with each moment, God is calling toward a consistent vision for the wholeness and flourishing of the world, but the advance toward that future involves many embodiments in the dance with the world.

The process of becoming moment by moment means that our self and vocation are in constant process as well. Vocation is not a thing we possess but rather the shape of our continual responses to God and our relationships (human and nonhuman). Consistency and continuity of responses in the past and of anticipation of responses in the future can mislead us into objectifying vocation into something to "have"—a situation of "misplaced concreteness" in process philosophy terms. The implication is that over our life-span the embodiments of vocation (responses and partnerships with God) will change and evolve, but that fluidity may be completely overshadowed by a narrow focus on the trajectory between those embodiments.

When vocational stability is not held in tension with vocational evolution (i.e., the arising of vocation in each moment and place), vocation becomes a station or function to hold. When vocational evolution is not held in tension with vocational stability, we risk losing the contributions and coherence of prior experience, learning, gifts, and graces to our current partnership with God.

The tension of vocational continuity and evolution seems to include other tensions as well. One is the tension between vocation in the present and anticipated vocation in the future. Often this tension collapses as persons tend to see vocation as a movement into a future role at the expense of partnership with God in the present. If we cannot be in partnership with God in the present, do we really expect to do so in the future? We encounter God concretely in the place of the present. A second tension is between the passion(s) underlying vocation and the forms in which vocation is embodied. In a healthy tension, one's vocational passion(s) take many forms, even though one form may be central. For example, one's passion for reconciliation may take the form of pastoral ministry, but it can also be embodied in parenting, friendships, and citizenship. Overemphasizing passion can make vocation vague and unrecognizable. Emphasizing the forms and embodiment of vocation can limit vocation to one aspect of one's life, which often puts the other aspects of life in competition with that particular embodiment of vocation. A third tension is closely related to the second: the tension between vocational organization and vocational freedom, particularly in the context of the church where we encounter clergy (pastors, chaplains, deacons, etc.), professional lay staff, and laity. Emphasizing vocational organization may lead to a rigid ecclesiology with everyone in their place. Emphasizing vocational freedom may lead to ineffective chaos. Either emphasis can lead to conflict. We need dynamic and transparent structures that create vocational empowerment and freedom.

God's participation in each moment of becoming means that everyone experiences the opportunity to be in vocation—we need only say yes. If nothing can separate us from the love of God, nothing can separate us from the lure/call of God. So, vocation is not reserved for clergy, not just for those mature in faith or human development (vocation is intergenerational), and not just the saved and sanctified. The depth and consistency of responsiveness to partnership with God may differ significantly between these groups, but being summoned by God remains constant for them all.

Personally Based ⟷ Contextually Evoked

A third tension in understanding vocation is between vocation as personally based and contextually evoked. Many discernment processes related to vocation (and career) make extensive use of various inventories to assess individual attributes. They may cover personality types, strengths, spiritual gifts, aptitudes, psychological dynamics, conflict management styles, learning styles, intercultural competency, multiple intelligences, and the like. These are very important and helpful in understanding oneself and the capacities one brings to partnership with God. Their use also indicates the extent to which we understand vocation as rooted in the person.

The roles of context and place in vocational discernment are often indirect. In the spirit of Frederick Buechner's description of vocation as the intersection of passion and need, context tends to enter as the arena of need.[5] Context also enters as consideration is given to the formative community's recognition of an individual's gifts and graces. If one's vocation becomes associated with a profession (religious or secular), typically the individual leaves the context of formative calling to pursue education. A major challenge in professional education is effective contextual education: helping students function in a context. Somewhat ironically, this kind of vocational education typically takes a person out of his or her context.

The tension between personally based and contextually evoked vocation shapes how we perceive our personal uniqueness. A beloved biblical passage is Isaiah 43:1—"I have called you by name, you are mine." Vocation here is a cherished gift of one's personal relationship with God, and indeed it is since it reflects God's calling us into being in every moment—uniqueness of vocation is personally based. Individual uniqueness arises from contextually rooted vocation as well. God calls us into being each moment from the webs of relationships in which we find ourselves—our places. No two people exist in the same set of relationships, whether in the mode of receiving blessings or of giving service—uniqueness of vocation is contextually rooted.

When the personal base of vocation is not held in tension with contextually rooted vocation, context and place become backdrops to individual action—persons seek a place to express their gifts; persons bring their vocation to a place (gift or baggage). In this framework, the task is to either find a location in which a pre-formed vocation fits in or can be "contextualized" (adapted) to a setting. Here, we risk conflating personal needs with needs of others and distorting vocation into subjective spirituality or, worse yet, a personality cult. When the contextual evocation of vocation is not held in tension with personally based vocation, the demands of context and place overshadow passion, and vocation can become sacrificial duty. Here, we risk numbness to prophetic voices, ambivalence to the stranger, and disinterest in confirming giftedness.

Several other tensions are wrapped up in the larger tension between personally based and contextually evoked vocation. The first tension is in some ways a paraphrasing of the main tension: it is the tension between grace received by individuals in their spiritual journey and prevenient grace interwoven in places. Certainly, individuals bring gifts and graces to contexts and place, but we should never be seduced into thinking we are the ones bringing grace to a place; God proceeds well in advance of our arrival. A second tension is between being an actor and being a recipient in vocation—there is a reciprocity with others in a place. If service is not held in tension with receiving, we become dismissive of others' abilities and thus disempower them. Losing sight of receiving can also miss that study, prayer, and Sabbath are forms of vocation, not ancillary to it. A third tension is between individuals and communities. In this tension, we have the issue of the interplay of the vocations of individuals and the vocations of their communities as a whole, as well as the issue of the place communities have in confirming ways individuals may embody their vocations. This is closely connected to the interplay of local culture and doctrines of ecclesiology.

Neglected Components of Vocation

Major Enlivening Tensions	Neglected Component(s)
Following in discipleship ⇔ Partnering in vocation	Partnership with God
Vocational continuity ⇔ Vocational evolution	Vocation and identity in process
Personally based vocation ⇔ Contextually evoked vocation	Vocation arising from context/place

A REVISED UNDERSTANDING OF VOCATION

The work of James Fowler influences many discussions of vocation.[6] Stemming from his work on faith development, Fowler came to recognize that *vocation* was how he thought about the vision a particular faith community held for the end of human development, while he used the term *faith* in reference to a universal human process of meaning-making. In *Becoming Adult, Becoming Christian*, Fowler defined vocation as the "response a person makes of their total self to the address of God and to partnership with God."[7] Later, in *Weaving the New Creation,* he gave a more extended definition:

> Vocation, as set forth here, involves a process of commitment, and ongoing discerning of one's gifts and giftedness in community, and of finding the means and settings in which those gifts—in all the dimensions of our living—can be placed at the disposal of the One who calls us into being and partnership.[8]

Vocation is partnership with God's work in and for the world within particular places. The call to partnership comes from God, but the places we dwell evoke it. *Rooted in the concrete elements of a place, vocation responds to God's vision for forming relationships reflective of God's Kin-dom.* Vocation is a relational and communal way of being in the world animated by a variety of passions. Redemptive and prevenient grace makes both our giftedness and limitations resources for vocation. Over time and across the places of daily life and our lives, we come to recognize a pattern and trajectory to the forms of our responsive partnerships. Partnership is possible at any point in life, but it grows in depth and consistency with education and nurture.

We partner with God's work in and for the world.

Partnership names a relationship. It does not mean we are on equal footing with God or that God's sovereignty is diminished. The witness of scripture and the saints is that God chooses to work with and through human agents. Knowing the heart and will of God, the one with whom we partner, is a fundamental task for our journeys and our ministries of discipleship.

God calls, but place evokes vocation.

In the ongoing process of creation, God continually calls us into being and partnership. The graces and needs of place also evoke us into being and partnership—we are the histories and relationships that place gathers. The complex ways that these graces and needs come together in both oppressive and liberative ways (intersectionality) puts a claim on us.

Vocation is a way of relationally being in the world.

With God and place evoking identity and vocation, responsiveness to others (service) is constitutive of who we are and not just an expression of spirituality. Vocation is an expression of topophilia involving love, empathy, and care for place. *Such care means giving forms to relationships that are redemptive and life-generating—a relational integration of the Great Commission and the Great Commandment. This relational form-giving work is central to vocation and is a reason that place is central to vocation.* Often we think of vocation as responding to a need of others, but the relational nature of vocation demands mutuality where we receive as well. Without mutuality in vocation, others become merely the objects of our work.

Vocation weaves together personal and communal.

We are persons-in-community, so our interconnectedness means that our vocations arise together—God is calling the one and the many at the same time. In this light, we can understand place as a web of vocations. Using vocation as a way to make ourselves feel like unique individuals, different from the rest, rends this web. While our vocational distinctiveness has roots in our personal histories and relationship with God, distinctiveness also arises from the uniqueness of one's location in place. No one shares the same history or locus of relationships in place as I, nor the same opportunities for collaborating in communal vocation.

Vocation in community raises issues of organization, roles, accountability, and authority—matters of ecclesiology beyond the scope of this project. Here, vocation falls on rocky ground because we do not have adequate ways of talking about the range of ways Christians are in partnership with God. Too often we limit vocation to those who are ordained. We become confused in the categories of professional, volunteer/worker, staff, certified in fill-in-the-blank, and so on. We must find ways to create order that promote freedom of vocational imagination. One starting point is to see baptism and confirmation as rituals of ordination into partnership with God generally (not just initiation into membership) and the ordination of clergy as extending that vocation into unique forms of leadership and responsibility.

Vocation involves various forms of animating passions.

The etymology of passion goes back to the Latin *passionem*, which denotes suffering and enduring. In Christian theology, it was mainly associated with the sufferings of Christ. During the mid-thirteenth century, connotations of strong emotion and desire arose. The suffering in passion is not a masochistic one. It is pain that emerges when we care about others, communities, and the world—when we see brokenness and injustice. It is also the pain of birthing and creating. Emotion is something closer to the center of our selves than mere feelings. Passion—suffering, endurance, emotion, and desire—is a dynamo for who we are. Without it we just go through the motions; assignments, graduation, ordination, and licensing become hoops through which to jump.

We experience joy and bliss when we are in harmony with our truest self—when we do "what I was born to do." We suffer when we face aspects of our own brokenness (whether from our choices or actions of others) and the brokenness of our places. The desire to alleviate suffering can motivate the work of redemption, healing, mercy, and justice. We have longings to pursue powerful visions of the ways things could be—life questions of "what if?"[9] We fall into awe and wonder as we encounter beauty, creativity, love, courage, and the face of God in the world. Sometimes passion is the compulsion to do what must be done in the face of fear, hardship, pain, and danger.

Passions are poured into particular forms of vocational activity that manifest across all that one does and all the places one dwells. Passion for beauty, wholeness, justice, or faithfulness finds embodiment in various ways in offices, clinics, churches, schools, recreation, homes, and public spaces. Collapsing vocation to one aspect of our life pits that aspect over against the rest of our life, thereby creating a divided self.

Vocation is a grace holding together our giftedness and limitations.

In choosing to work with and through human agents, God gets a mixed bag. While our weaknesses and failings do make us reliant on God's strength, we should not let this fact diminish our responsiveness to partnership with God. Our limitations are not just the results of sin and brokenness—we are simply finite creatures. Our capacities for partnership vary because of developmental stage, abilities, health, resources, and the like. God's redemptive creativity allows God to use whatever we have, wherever we are. In using our limitations, God redeems them in vocation, thus making them a grace to accompany our gifts. We also encounter a form of prevenient grace as we encounter *I Am—Place*[10] in the places we dwell. If place is the ground of calling, it is also the ground of grace. God does not call without liberating and empowering, nor blessing us with co-workers. Partnership is a possibility at any point and in any place of life.

Vocation is a growing freedom of responsiveness.

Being in vocation across the whole journey of life and discipleship only requires the capacity to respond. Even taking the next breath is a response to God's call to life! Hopefully, the depth, consistency, and freedom of response to partnership with God's work in the world grows over time. Such growth can happen when developmental stages, education, and discipleship make knowledge, skills, and attitudes available for vocation and place. Sometimes we must begin by removing the obstacles to vocational growth created by personal choices and social injustice. Growth in vocation is a process of sanctification as we experience freedom for deepening consistency to say yes in the moment to God's lure of partnership. Vocation is not deferred to adulthood, abandoned at retirement, or blocked by disabilities. While the robustness and consistency of service may vary, the option to be in responsive partnership with God's work in the world does not.

Vocation connects past and future in the now of place.

We tend to use a future tense in the way we speak of vocation—it is something out there that we pursue. On the other hand, we can fall prey to thinking that the ways we have been in partnership during the past define our vocation. While there is anticipation and preparation for vocation in the future and there is faithfulness in the vocation of the past, the now of place is where our vocation is experienced and embodied. If we cannot be in partnership with God in the present, how can we expect to be in the future?

SUMMARY

The first step in responding to failed vocational imagination is looking at matters of purpose—God's relationship with the world and God's work in the world. My general understanding of God's work is that of gathering the world into being and forming relationships that provide fullness of life and the Spirit. We partner with God in gathering graces, redeeming brokenness, and finding wholeness reflective of the Kin-dom of God.

This chapter takes the second step of exploring our assumptions about the nature of vocation itself. Expanding our understandings about vocation addresses the problem that too often our vocational imagination is limited—one of the causes of failed vocational imagination.

A review of theological tensions influencing our views of vocation set an agenda for vocational imagination and theology. We need to

- Embrace human giftedness and human brokenness

- Engage personal and social holiness where we dwell

- Trust God's presence in places we dwell and the larger world

- Draw upon the witnesses of scripture and tradition and be open to the One who makes all things new

- Utilize diverse ways to encounter God as guide and to recognize God's involvement in the world

- Draw upon the discerning wisdom and empowering support of others

- Connect discipleship with expressions of respectful witness and compassionate service

Three aspects of vocation need integration into our thinking about vocation. One is that vocation involves active *partnership* with God and not just following. A second is that vocation is a *process* in which the forms of our vocations change over time and in different places—vocation is not a thing to possess. The third is that *vocation emerges from place* just as much as it does from an individual.

These aspects appear in a concise definition of vocation as a *process of partnership* with God's work in and for the world within and *evoked by particular places*. Expanding on this definition involves several important features of vocation:

- Partnership with God's work

- God calls, but place evokes vocation

- Vocation is a way of relationally being in the world

- Vocation weaves together personal and communal

- Vocation involves various forms of animating passions

- Vocation is a grace holding together our giftedness and limitations

- Vocation is a growing freedom of responsiveness

- Vocation connects past and future in the now of place

In the next chapter, we will begin rethinking assumptions about place to understand more fully its role in evoking and forming vocation—the second cause of failed vocational imagination.

FOR REFLECTION

Personal Perspective

1. What aspects and assumptions about vocation have caused you to question your sense of being in vocation? What would give you peace about your sense of vocation?

2. Review the theological themes and tension in the chart on pages 42–43. How do you hold together the tensions in each theological theme and what are the implications for your

understanding of vocation? Which theological theme, if any, is more influential to you than others?

3. How do each of the assumptions about vocation broaden your vocational imagination and help your sense of vocation?

   a. Vocation involves partnership.

   b. Vocation is dynamic and evolving—not a thing to possess.

   c. Vocation is evoked by places and routes.

4. What aspects of the definition of vocation in this chapter do you find useful or challenging?

Leadership Perspective

5. What aspects and assumptions about vocation do you see causing persons to question their sense of being in vocation?

6. How are you helping persons to think theologically about vocation…to be practical everyday theologians?

7. What do you understand as creating passivity in the discipleship of those you lead?

8. How do you think about the relationship between discipleship and vocation?

9. How is your vocation evoked by the place(s) you lead? How is your vocation evoked in places where you are not in leadership?

10. What aspects of the definition of vocation in this chapter reinforce or cause you to rethink the ways you teach about and equip persons for vocation?

Congregational Perspective

11. What does the congregation explicitly and implicitly teach about the nature of vocation?

12. What theological commitments shape the way the congregation views the vocation of individuals and the congregation?

13. How has the vocation of the congregation changed over time?

14. To what extent is the congregation connected to its place and how does this shape its sense of vocation?

15. What aspect of the definition of vocation in this chapter might help the congregation reflect on its collective vocation?

Chapter 4

GATHERING AND EMERGING: PLACE AND RELATIONSHIPS

WHERE ON EARTH AM I?

The Mass had ended and I sat in the pew bewildered. *Where on earth am I?* I thought. Earlier in the service the priest had publicly introduced me as someone studying the congregation's youth ministry. That was before his homily in which he made some comments critical of a group in the parish. It so happened that the leader of said group was also a leader of the gospel choir. This provided a platform and a mic, which he used to publicly shout down the priest after the homily. The experiences of the Mass created a church place I had never encountered, nor had I encountered a place like this congregation's parish. I was in a predominantly African-American Catholic parish near south central Los Angeles, seemingly a world away from Anderson, Indiana, where I grew up.

The only things I knew about the parish in LA were from a colleague who had contacts there and from the mass media reporting about that area of Los Angeles. My colleague's depictions helped convince me to spend the summer with the parish; the mass media depictions evoked the biases, fears, and naiveté instilled from my Anderson roots. The major streets in the parish looked as I imagined, but once on the side streets the neighborhood did not look that much different from many in Anderson. Certainly, there were many needs, but there were many assets as well. The congregation was active in the community through its members, ministries, and parochial school. Wisdom called for some street awareness, but it was far from the war zone shown on TV. Hospitality in the congregation was pervasive—whenever I felt uncomfortable, it was because of the baggage I brought to the place. A deep sense of connectedness with each other and with the place of the parish was also prevalent.

The public conflict during Mass naturally surfaced in many conversations over the subsequent weeks of my study. I learned that the congregation saw itself as a family. The passing of the peace during Mass was a carnival-like time of embraces and catching up with each other—even that morning after the shout down of the priest. Communion (Eucharist) contributed to a sense of unity between persons, despite their differences. I learned that about once a year some kind of "excitement" like what I witnessed happened, and people came to expect something transformative to result. One person explained that everyone expected conflicts because when people hold deep values, friction around such things happens. The lives of congregants intertwined with each other in the larger community. Significant persons in one's life were claimed as kin and given titles of aunt, uncle, sister, and brother. Collectively these dynamics fostered a "we are family" mindset. One person explained that the congregation was like a "real" family that had fights and then made up. When conflicts arose, the idea and connections of being family lessened urges to leave.

Our perspectives about God's work in the world and the nature of vocation itself shape vocational imagination. Place is deeply intertwined with both these concepts. In reference to God, place is where we concretely experience the nature of God's relationship with the world. We will also see that the gathering power of place and the forms of relationships in place have similarities with God's gathering and relationship-forming work. In reference to vocation, place is where we concretely experience the call of God—not only into our vocation but into our being. Our identities arise from what place gathers, and in turn place is the arena of our partnership with God, shaping relationships to foster flourishing of life and the Spirit.

This chapter will present a definition of place and elaborate on several aspects of that definition. In brief, place is *a process of gathering* groups of people, creatures, plants, climate, and physical structures into a web of relationships—it is our relational way of being in the world. After the work of defining place, we will address three problematic perceptions of place needing correction: that place is static, that place is parochial, and that place is anthropocentric. In a manner similar to that taken in chapter 3, we will reflect on several theological themes that influence assumptions about place.

This LA congregation was much more than a group of people worshipping God and serving others. God gathered them. The sanctuary, parish hall, parochial school, rectory, and the larger geographic parish gathered them as well. Many practices gave form to the relationships between those gathered—Eucharist, passing the peace, caring for youth and children, music, retreat ministries, community action, kinship, and, yes, even conflict. These practices included a sense of anticipation that God was showing up in their midst to provide guidance and purpose. The deep bonds of the relationships formed arose from responsiveness to partnership with God and to assumptions about being interconnected. They were very much engaged in forming relationships so that life and the Spirit could flourish—place-making.

RELATIONALITY

Place is a particular collection of formative relationships rather than merely a location in space. It is the web of relationships from which we come to be and to which we contribute. Place is a fundamental way to experience and understand human, ecological, physical, and spiritual relationships. We cannot exist apart from place—we become who we are from what places gather and from our ongoing encounters with God (*I Am—Place*) in place.[1] The call to partnership with God comes from God, but the places we dwell and routes we travel evoke it. *Vocation responds to God's vision for forming relationships in place and on routes reflective of God's Kin-dom.* Vocation is a relational and communal way of being in the world.

I think there are at least two reasons place is overlooked in relationships. One reason is that relationships with friends, colleagues, and family tend to span particular places and endure over time so place does not seem essential to them. A second reason is that we think of relationships primarily as interpersonal, to the exclusion of relationships with social, ecological, and physical aspects of our lives.

Yet, place plays an important role in our experience of enduring interpersonal relationships. The senses significantly influence memories and intensity of interpersonal relationships. The sights, sounds, feelings, smells, and tastes of places are integral to experiences and their significance. When we remember experiences, aspects of the places in which they happened tend to come as well. This is not just because senses aid memory. It is also because, in addition to the interpersonal aspects, the social, ecological, physical, and spiritual relationships in place are contributing to and forming experience. For many years as part of teaching about faith development, I have asked persons to write faith journeys including important people and places. More recently, I ask persons to write about places with attention to relationships and faith. Helpful as the faith journeys have been to persons, what these reflections about place evoke is much more powerful and emotional.

If place is all about relationships, then why not keep things simple and just talk about relationships? The reason is to press our awareness of the rich web of relationships that shape us and of how God entrusts that web to our care. Place is that web of interpersonal, social, ecological, spiritual, and physical relationships.

A WORKING DEFINITION OF PLACE

Place is a process of gathering groups of people, creatures, plants, climate, and physical structures into a web of relationships. Place also shapes the way we imagine and make meaning of this localized web and our position in it—our relational way of being in the world. Habits in the process of forming relationships between what is gathered give places their character. Places are full of assets, hindrances, and graces for flourishing.

A Process and History of Gathering Events

We sometimes talk about certain locations as "gathering places," but gathering is a key dynamic of *every* place. Edward Casey explains,

> *Places gather*... places gather things in their midst—where "things" connote various animate and inanimate entities. Places also gather experiences and histories, even languages and thoughts. Think only of what it means to go back to a place you know, finding it full of memories and expectations, old things and new things, the familiar and strange, and much more besides. What else is capable of this massively diversified holding action?... The power belongs to place itself, and it is a power of gathering.[2]

The things that a place gathers change constantly through new experiences, seasons, evolution, decay, and movement. This means that the act of gathering by place must happen over and over again. Each gathering is an assembly for the moment. As Casey notes, "A place is more an *event* than a *thing*."[3] This gathering is not just what is currently in a physical space. Place is an event of gathering the history of a space over time. Our experience of the continuity and discontinuity in how a place gathers gives place its character.[4]

A Way of Making the World Meaningful

Place is more than a simple geographic location or area. Place is a fundamental way of making meaning from localized human and nonhuman relationships. If asked where we are from or where we dwell, our response is not a set of coordinates—a city is not a place because it is locatable by GPS. Our answers involve a name that stirs up meanings for those acquainted with it in terms of geography, demographics, history, culture, economics, personal connections, or some other category. If another is unacquainted with our city, or reflects what we take to be a misrepresentation of it, we explain the meanings of the relationships we have with the people, land, creatures, and the natural and built environment. Place enables us to give meaning to a local set of relationships. Tim Cresswell describes place as "how we make the world meaningful and the way we experience the world. Place, at a basic level, is space invested with meaning in the context of power."[5] Place, in contrast to space or mere location, is neither an objective thing in itself nor a characteristic of things in the world but rather "an aspect of the way we choose to think about it—what we decide to emphasize and what we decide to designate as unimportant."[6]

The Stuff of What We Are

Place gathers and presents to us the raw material for constructing our identity and vocation—we are the histories and relationships that place gathers. We take what place offers and weave it into who we are in ways that are novel, conformist, or a bit of both. It is in the relationships gathered by place that we continually come into being and contribute to the becoming of others—both place and that which it holds are in processes of becoming at the same time. Cresswell notes, "Place is the raw material for the creative production of identity rather than an *a priori* label of identity. Place provides the conditions of possibility for creative social practice."[7] Jeff Malpas clearly depicts subjectivity as the foundation of individual subjectivity: "One does not first have a subject that apprehends certain features of the world in terms of the idea of place; instead, the structure of subjectivity is given in and through the structure of place."[8]

The connections between identity and place that Cresswell and Malpas describe seem consistent with process theology's view of the self. In this perspective, the self is a continuity of individual moments of experience, a continuous process of becoming moment by moment. We arise in a moment; the moment ends and we arise again in the next moment. In each moment of experience, we sense our past and that of the world about us both human and nonhuman. It makes sense to speak of place as the gathering of what we sense. This means we are radically interrelated with others and the world. We arise along with the world, we arise in a web of relationships. God participates in each moment of experience of each part of the world offering, luring, propositioning with a way to weave together our past and our relationships. That proposition from God offers the most redemptive and life-giving option for us individually and the world as a whole in the moment. God's offering is not coercive, it is a luring—there is radical freedom in each moment to reject in whole or part the proposition from God. Despite such radical freedom, the reality is the weight of past experiences and decisions creates a trajectory, inertia, habituation to replicate prior ways of being. Once a moment of experience concrescences, it contributes to the next moment of experience for the self and other to repeat the process of coming into being. The assemblage of elements (creatures, plants, land, climate, built environment, culture, habitat) that constitute place are internally related and are co-constituting. Any one element arises from its relationships with other elements in a place. At the same time place is the assemblage of these elements. In working with each moment, God is luring toward a consistent vision for the wholeness and flourishing of the world, but the advance toward that future involves many embodiments in the dance with the world.

Roots, Routes, and Nested Places

In proposing correctives to negative assumptions about place, I argue that while place endures over time, it is also dynamic; and while place is localized, it is also open and interconnected. These correctives point to the ways that identity and vocation have roots in particular places, while at the same time they transcend particular places as the routes of life take us between places. Over the course of life, we dwell in different places. Within daily life, many of us move between the places of work, school, home, marketplace, and play. We move between different cultural places in privileged and disadvantaged ways. Networks of family, friends, and associations may cause us to travel between places. We encounter both the roots and the routes of identity and vocation in relation to places.

Formed by Practices, Power, and Intersectionality

Social and relational systems shape the meanings that transform space into place through narratives and practices. Practices enculturate us into a *habitus*, or lasting dispositions that function "at every moment as a matrix of perceptions, appreciations, and actions."[9] Places are constantly under construction through practices involving power, agency, and social systems.[10] Practices condition but do not determine how persons experience and construct place—the freedom to improvise and practice resiliency is also part of how practices work.

Hierarchies and power mark the terrain of social and relational systems as well. When people do not conform to imposed norms, they are viewed as transgressors and labeled "out of place."[11] The terrain of power in place is complex and many layered—we lose track of where we are when we focus on a single layer of gender, race, class, or ability. Place is an encounter with intersectionality. The primacy of place means that "[place] is a force that cannot be reduced to the social, the natural, or the cultural. It is, rather, a phenomenon that brings these worlds together and, indeed, in part produced them."[12]

CORRECTIVES FOR UNDERSTANDING PLACE

We need to address three commonly held assumptions about place: place is static, place is parochial, and place is anthropocentric.

Assumptions About Place

Problematic Assumptions about Place	Corrective Aspect
Place is static.	Place is dynamic.
Place is parochial.	Place is interconnected.
Place is anthropocentric.	Place is inclusive habitat.

Place is dynamic.

In a contemporary world obsessed with change, the pervasiveness of the assumption that place is static is odd. A static sense of place might arise from several sources. Longing for a sense of rootedness may cause persons to emphasize place as a steady point of reference and risks romanticizing notions of one's origins. Place can also be construed as a retreat from the change-fatigue of dealing with society. Our propensity for short-term thinking can mask the longer-term character of change occurring in place. Trying to maintain static harbors leads to ever shrinking micro-places with homogeneity that creates myopia to awareness of change and to the presence of others. Perhaps viewing place as static reflects the ways we deny our own fluidity and evolutionary processes. Do we even assume that idealized places such as the garden of Eden and heaven are static—or as a Talking Heads song says, "Heaven is a place where nothing ever happens?"[13]

As vocation and identity are in process (change over time) yet have trajectories, place is in process and has a consistency that can be confused with stasis. We risk making place into a thing rather than a process. People and creatures move about and through place, as do water and air. Living things come to life, grow, decline, and perish. Buildings and infrastructure arise and age. Land and environment change. Much as individuals arise, places are the continuities of ongoing gathering events. All that is in a place arises from and in response to what is gathered together by place. In turn, the interrelationships give rise to place. Place is a dance in which: a) the "raw material for the creative production of identity [and] . . . creative social practice"[14] are gathered; b) individuals arise in response to relationships and God's lure; and c) the experience and resources of those individuals are gathered into the next iteration of place. In process terms, place is a web of becomings with continuity over time.

Place is interconnected.

A parochial sense of place is intertwined with assuming place is static. US culture places much more value on being on a journey than dwelling in a place. The celebrated heroes of quests and adventures in classic mythologies (even Dorothy in *Wizard of Oz*) tend to bring their newfound identities and rewards home, but that is seldom the case today. Bias in favor of journey over dwelling is evident in metaphors of faith and spirituality—faith journeys, Jacob's ladder, Abraham's leaving home, and so on. To dwell, to live in place, for some smacks of narrowness, backwardness, dependency, and even failure. Youth are encouraged to leave places of origin to escape depressed economies, pursue careers, or just "find themselves." A good dose of classism exists in this dynamic as well.[15]

Place can seem parochial if we assume that one place is separated from others. Yet places are interconnected with each other in various ways. One might immediately think of the "global village" fostered by communications and media. However, at least two other factors interconnect places. One is that the boundaries between places can be uncertain by virtue of their vagueness, overlap, or embeddedness in each other. The second factor is that things (people, goods, species, weather, water, air, etc.) move between places. Some would argue that places are created by the habits of movement that members of a place routinely follow.[16] Consider how your movements at work, school, church, and over the course of a day contribute to your sense of place in these locations and in daily life. Doreen Massey's work also suggests that attending to routes as well as roots in relation to place helps fend off parochialism. I have argued that people and places are in process—the histories of their many ongoing experiences and gatherings respectively. One or a few places in our histories gather experiences in profound ways that root our identities. At the same time, our histories are routes through many places. The routes themselves, in addition to the particular significant places, shape who we are. We and the others about us bring both our routes and roots as place gathers us in the present.

Place is inclusive habitat.

We need to see place as an inclusive habitat benefitting spiritual, human, and environmental flourishing. Anthropocentric assumptions about place discount the ways ecological and physical spheres interact with the human. By adopting these assumptions, we diminish the range of our formative relationships with the world and dismiss the consequences of our actions on the world. In a simplistic form of anthropocentrism, we relegate place and environment to being an inert backdrop to human activity. Another form of anthropocentrism—with harmful consequences—assumes place and environment are only valuable in relation to their contribution to humans. Place is inclusive of ecological and physical dimensions, so to the degree that anthropocentrism diminishes these, anthropocentrism diminishes places in which we all come to exist.

APPROACHING PLACE THEOLOGICALLY

As with the concept of vocation, we understand place within faith communities shaped by church traditions and theological dispositions within them. However, on its own terms, place is not yet a common category for theological reflection, although this is beginning to change.[17] Aspects of place surface as part of theological reflection on topics such as community, public, "the world," context, ecology, and parish. Land and place are very important themes in Jewish thought. Place is connected to memory of God's actions, which is a significant feature of Jewish understandings of faith. Themes of the promised land are prominent in the formation of a Jewish people.[18] Land and place are also very important to themes in First Nations, postcolonial, and eco-womanist theologies. The connections between identity and place are essential to theological reflection of the dynamics and experience of diaspora. Place surfaces as we consider holy sites, shrines, memorials, the "thin places" in Celtic spirituality, and sacred space (including debates about seeker-sensitive buildings).

Here I would like to offer some theological categories that help engage assumptions about how we view place theologically. Most of these are the same used for vocation with different foci, yet the need to address tensions within them and to consider a range of them remains.

Human Nature

Theological assumptions about the goodness and corruption of human nature tend to flow into perspectives about place, which demonstrates our anthropocentric tendencies. In terms of the natural aspects of place, the fallenness of humanity often is extended to the fall of creation and place as well—humanity's fall broke *all* of creation, as suggested in Romans 8:22-23.[19] Sometimes creation appears as a sphere of innocence in contrast to human fallenness and as suffering at the hands of humanity. In terms of the aspects of place created by humanity, a more direct ambivalence about the goodness of place exists. Emphasizing human corruption leads to place as being "the world," a way station on the path to eternity, or part of the social basis for original sin. Valuing human goodness provides the opportunity to recognize the beauty and blessing of human creativity and community. *Our imagination of place needs to embrace the blessings and brokenness of place so we may recognize the obstacles and graces for flourishing where we dwell.*

Whether human nature is essentially one of interrelatedness with or independence from others is an important tension that place creatively holds. Thinking of human nature as interrelated with others undergirds the notion that place evokes us into identity and vocation. At the same time, place evokes a response that is uniquely ours. In our interrelatedness with place, we are conditioned by what place gathers but not determined by that, as we give form to the relationships in place. *Our imagination of place needs to reflect our being made in the image of a communal, interrelated God (trinitarian).*

Transformation

The theological tension in vocation between transformation initiated on the social level, and that initiated on the individual level, plays out differently in relation to place. At first glance, it seems that engaging place is a matter of social transformation. However, the dynamics of place inherently involve personal *and* social transformation. We exist in the interplay between how place calls us into personal identity and how we in turn give form to social and ecological relationships in place. We are place-making as we form relationships in light of the Kin-dom—and given our interdependence—transforming individuals as well. We are agents of place-making but not the authors of it. Place-making is done in response to and in partnership with God (*I Am—Place*), the One who constantly calls us and place into ongoing re-creation. *Our imagination of place needs to empower us for place-making and way-making work incorporating social, personal, and ecological spheres of life reflective of the Kin-dom of God.*

70

God and World

My assumptions about place emphasize God's immanence and incarnation in relationship with the world. God is at work in the heart of place—place evokes, but God calls us into being and partnership. However, the tension with God's transcendence should not be lost. Claims about God's immanence in place must face the realities of places filled with abuse, pain, suffering, and violence. Are these signs that God must be distant in order not to compromise God's holiness? Can a place be so broken that surely God must be absent? My sense is that sin embodied in place is not the last word. God in place does not mean God's entrapment in place. God is more than any one place and transcends place as God continually and redemptively works to re-create places in light of the transcending Kin-dom of God. *Our imagination of place needs to trust God's presence in places we dwell and trust in God's greater movement.*

Revelation

Questions of revelation and place are similar to those of God and world. My assumptions about God's immanence in place encourage us to expect God's self-disclosure in place—an example of *general revelation* about God through place. Such revelation might provide a broad insight about God or involve a sense of the Holy Spirit personally addressing us. In addition to general revelation, we also need *special revelation* through witnesses of scripture and tradition. The contrast between these two forms of revelation fosters critical consciousness in processes of discernment. Scripture and tradition provide references for recognizing the brokenness and giftedness of place. The movement of God in place provides a reference for engaging the bounds of scripture and tradition. *Our imagination of place needs to raise our attentiveness to God's disclosure in place and foster dialogue with the witnesses of scripture and tradition.*

Trinity

Generally, the theme of the Trinity as a reflection of the communal nature of God resonates with place as a locus of deep interrelatedness.

Whether the interrelatedness of a place reflects sanctity is another matter. The economic expression of the Trinity offers us more focused connections with place. In continuing to call us and place into being (creation), continuing to lead transformation of our relationships in place toward those of the Kin-dom of God (redemption), and continuing to sustain flourishing of faith and life, the Trinity is active in place. *Our imagination of place needs to help us recognize the work of the Trinity in place and ways we are called into partnership with that work.*

Church

In considering the church, whether as the body of Christ or as a human institution, its particular incarnations are places (both as churches and parishes). The church is intertwined with place as its rituals, practices, narratives, resources, and processes intermingle with the elements of place. In some ways, this reflects the constant contextualization of the church, but it also reflects an embodied sacramentality and spirituality of place. As with the Great Commandment and Great Commission, the question is to what degree *all* that place gathers is included in the community of the church. Is the church an overarching way of thinking about the area of a congregation (parish), or is the church limited to the particular location of the congregation? *Our imagination of place needs to help us discern the sacramental and vocational incarnations of the church in particular places.*

Church Mission

Because we encounter God (*I Am—Place*), neighbors, and other creatures within the setting of place, it provides a powerful framework for holding together the tension between the Great Commandment and the Great Commission. By also gathering creation and built environments, place also broadens our understandings of the Great Commandment and the Great Commission past anthropocentric concerns to embrace all of creation. *Our imagination of place needs to expand our sense of mission to include all that place gathers.*

Eschatology

How we religiously imagine the trajectory of history and its end are part of eschatology. Monotheistic religions tend to have a linear sense of time flowing into the future toward some ultimate goal such as "judgment day," "eternal glory in heaven," or the full realization of the Kin-dom of God. As such, a goal receives increasingly more emphasis, a tension arises between life seen as a journey into the future and life as dwelling in the present. In extreme forms, the metaphor of a journey can displace us and make us aliens and refugees in our own world. *Our imagination of place needs to enable us to embrace the roots that the places we dwell offer and the routes we take between places as vital aspects of our spirituality and vocations.*

Theological Themes and Tensions

Theological Theme	Theological Tension			Place Issue
Human Nature	Good but often misses the mark	⇔	Corrupted and embedded in sin	Place as good or corrupted
	Communal	⇔	Individual	Place as local relationships Degree of anthropo-centrism
Transformation	Intersectionality	⇔	Individual Issues	Place overcoming dualisms
God and World	Immanence	⇔	Transcendence	Place overcoming dualisms
Incarnation	Material	⇔	Spirit	Place overcoming dualisms
Creation	Ongoing	⇔	Completed	Place in process
Revelation	General	⇔	Special	Place as a locus of revelation

Trinity	Creator—Redeemer—Sustainer		Place made in the image of interrelated Trinity Trinity's relation to place and creation
Church	Body of Christ	⇔ Human Institution	Does the body of Christ include place
	Gathering of Individuals	⇔ Parish	Community
Church Mission	Great Commandment	⇔ Great Commission	People and creation
Eschatology	Dwelling	⇔ Journey	Roots and routes

SUMMARY

I have proposed that God's work involves continually gathering the world into being and forming relationship that provide fullness of life and the Spirit—in essence gathering and forming the world in light of the Kin-dom of God. Broadening our understanding of vocation involves embracing vocation as active partnership with God, as a process rather than a thing, and as emerging from places.

Place plays an important role in God's relationship with the world, in the work of God, and in our identity and vocation. Disconnecting vocation from place fuels failure of vocational imagination. This chapter sought to present a view of place to support robust vocation.

To grasp the significance of place, one must recognize that place is a particular gathering of formative relationships rather than merely a location in space. The power of place is its ability to gather. We can make analogies between the gathering power of place and the gathering power of God. An abridged definition depicts place as a process of gathering groups

74

of people, creatures, plants, climate, and physical structures into a web of relationships. This definition involves several important features. Place is

- A process and history of gathering events

- A way of making the world meaningful

- The stuff of what we are

- A combination of roots, routes, and nested places

- Formed by practices, power, and intersectionality

In addition to understanding that place is more than location, we need to correct misperceptions that place is static, parochial, and human-centered. Instead, we need to recognize ways that place is in process, nested in larger contexts, and a habitat of which humans are one part.

A review of theological tensions influencing our views of place set an agenda for vocational imagination and theology. Our vocational imagination needs to

- Embrace the blessings and brokenness of place

- Empower us for place-making and way-making work

- Trust God's presence in places we dwell and on routes we take

- Increase our attentiveness to God's disclosure in place

- Help us recognize the work of the Trinity in place

- Help us discern the sacramental and vocational incarnations of the church in particular places

- Expand our sense of mission to include all that place gathers—not just congregations

In the next chapter, we will address another component in the vocational mix—the person with whom God partners. Part of what place gathers is our personal history—our sense of who we are, our capacities, and our purposes in life.

FOR REFLECTION

Personal Perspective

1. Describe a time when you were aware of how a place gathered people and creation in a unique way. What about the physical and social aspects of that place formed relationships to give the gathering a particular character or spirit?

2. To what extent does place have positive and negative connotations for you? Why?

3. What aspects of the definition of place in this chapter do you find useful or challenging?

4. What do you think are the implications of gathering as a central feature of place?

5. How do each of the assumptions about place broaden the ways you view place?

   a. Place is dynamic.

   b. Place is interconnected.

   c. Place is inclusive habitat.

6. Review the theological themes and tension in the chart on pages 73–74. How do you hold together the tensions in each theological theme and what are the implications for your understanding of place? Which theological theme, if any, is more influential to you than others?

7. What connections between place and vocation are you beginning to recognize?

Leadership Perspective

8. What do you think are the implications of gathering as a central feature of place for your approach to leadership?

9. How do you understand the role of place in forming the community you lead?

10. How does place shape the relationships and character of the community?

11. How does place shape the way you teach and equip for discipleship, ministry, and vocation?

12. How does place make ecology and the environment part of discipleship, ministry, and vocation?

13. How are you helping persons to think theologically about place…to be practical everyday theologians?

14. What aspects of the definition of place in this chapter reinforce or cause you to rethink the ways you teach about and equip persons for discipleship and vocation?

15. How might you equip persons to be aware of and to engage the places they dwell?

Congregational Perspective

16. To what extent is the congregation aware of the church itself as a place? Why?

17. To what extent is the congregation aware and engaged with the place in which it is situated (its parish)? Why?

18. How does place shape the relationship of the congregation with its surroundings?

19. What are important times that the congregation gathers? What role does the particular place of gathering have on relationships? What practices of gathering are involved?

20. How has the place of the congregation changed over time and what caused those changes?

Chapter 5

WITH WHOM IS GOD PARTNERING? CAPACITIES AND STORIES IN VOCATION

I'M BACK. SO NOW WHAT?

It was the first class after being back from a yearlong sabbatical. The topic was the intersection of leading, educating, and forming communities. The first session of a class always has me wondering what kind of semester it will be. Will the dynamics of the class be engaging, "meh," or a long, hard slog? (I am reasonably sure students ask the same questions.) A teacher or leader has a lot of influence on a group, but place-making is work shared by all those gathered. I was also wondering about myself. My sabbatical came a couple years after stepping down from a five-year stint as academic dean. I had yet to sort out the dynamics of returning to the faculty and to figure out some larger dynamics within the school. How was I going to be connected with the school? How was the school claiming and gathering me?

The class was largely first-semester seminary students. It gathered persons across a wide theological spectrum (from Unitarian Universalists to evangelical Christians). Openly gay and lesbian students were present.

79

Although not present in a large number, there were students with Latino, African-American, African, Native American, and Korean heritages. Student ages ranged from recently out of college to persons with several decades more experience. A student passionate about how the church should serve persons with disabilities raised the awareness of the class, and we discovered how many others in the class had persons with disabilities in their lives. Various students faced some form of trauma from experiences in the military, home, congregations, or oppressive social systems. Some students had clear sets of goals for themselves, and others felt adrift but knew they were in the right place for now—they somehow belonged here.

We were intentional about the class as a particular place that gathered us and talked about being a learning community with practices of hearing each other into speech and beholding each other into visibility. I committed to making the class a safe place but made no promises about anyone's comfort. Taking each other seriously was also an important value—in an academic setting, this is the nearest experience to love one gets.

Each week, the class-place gathered us anew. We accomplished the learning outcomes for the class, though the routes there were not always what I intended. Some sessions were powerful and others needed a serious postmortem to see what went wrong. The powerful ones deeply connected matters of society, faith, and ministry with personal experience. Assignments asked people to reflect on places in their lives and I heard reports of the insights gained and the tears shed. We shared in laughter, music, art, liturgy, and a variety of learning methods.

In all this engagement with each other, we were authoring each other and ourselves—helping each other show up and learning about who we were as partners with God's work in the world. By the end of the class, I did not feel like a perfect teacher, but I did feel authentic—I felt myself. The class created a place for Randy to show up, a place of empowering grace.

Earlier in this book, we raised a fundamental theological question in navigating vocation and place: *What do we think God is doing in the world?* If we are in partnership with God's work in the world, we need to be aware of what God is doing. We must also ask ourselves—*Who are we in this partnership with God and what are we seeking?* Thus far, we have considered understandings of God's gathering work, vocation, and place. In this chapter we now look more closely at the nature of the self and capacities of the self for partnership with God. The capacities for partnership with God include faith, hope, love, integrity, agency, and mutuality. Because the self is constructed by narratives, vocational stories are important in forming vocational imagination. The robustness of vocation in a faith community depends on the richness of vocational stories held and valued in that community. Vocational narratives author identity and vocational imaginations.

ASSUMPTIONS ABOUT THE SELF IN RELATION TO PLACE

As I have addressed place, vocation, and intersectionality, I have also presented several assumptions about the nature of the self. A brief recap of these will help prepare for looking closely at the dynamics between the self, place, and vocation.

The self is a process, the continuity of individual moments of experience.

In process theology, the self is the continuity of individual moments of experience, a continuous process of becoming moment by moment. We arise in a moment, the moment ends, and we arise again in the next moment. In each moment of experience, we sense our past and that of the world about us—both human and nonhuman. It makes sense to speak of place as the gathering of what we sense. This means we are radically interrelated with others and the world. We arise along with the world, we arise in a web of relationships. God participates in each moment of experience of each part of the world offering, luring, propositioning with a way to weave together our past and our relationships. That proposition from God offers the most redemptive and life-giving option for us individually and the world as a whole in the moment. God's offering is not coercive—there is radical freedom in each moment to reject in whole or part the proposition from God. Despite such radical freedom, the reality is the weight of past experiences, and decisions create a trajectory, inertia, habituation to replicate prior ways of being. Once a moment of experience is complete, it contributes to the next moment of experience for the self and others, repeating the process of coming into being. The assemblage of elements (creatures, plants, land, climate, built environment, culture, habitat) that constitute place are internally related and are co-constituting. Any one element arises from its relationships with other elements in a place. At the same time, place is the assemblage of these elements. In working with each moment, God is luring us toward a consistent vision for the wholeness and flourishing of the world, but the advance toward that future involves many embodiments.

The nature of human experience is narrative.[1]

The continuity of the self in process is narrative. It is a way of understanding the self as episodic and fluid, while still having some degree of coherence. Our telling and retelling of life experiences through narratives is a process of becoming ourselves. With each retelling, there is a revaluing of moments of experience, which can be either destructive or redemptive. The moments of experience are ours, but we do not create the story lines connecting them *ex nihilo*. We draw upon narrative patterns from the communities and places in which we find ourselves—blending them into our self-understanding with a mix of conformity, novelty, and even hostility. There is no lack of resources for creating the stories of self. We encounter the story lines of the variety of places in which we move in daily life and over the course of our life span. Additionally, each place where we live and move holds many story lines—some predominate and some are muted; some liberate and some confine.

Part of what place gathers is our personal history—our sense of who we are and our purposes in life. Identity and vocational narratives hold together the experiences in our personal history. These narratives mark the trajectory of gifts and brokenness we bring to places. As places and our movements between them evoke us into being and vocation, they continually recreate these narratives in ways that succumb to the inertia of the past and yield to God's creative call.

Identity is a matter of belonging.

Finding a story line for identity within Christian traditions requires facing the questions of whose we are. We are creatures of God and we are creatures of place—the embodied human, ecological, physical, and spiritual relationships that constitute our identity. God is continually offering us creatively redemptive story lines in each moment that provide us identity and purpose amidst the relationships in the places we dwell and between which we travel. These story lines are mediated by the Spirit and the accumulated witnesses cradled in sacred texts and traditions.

The self is hybrid.

Hybridity deals with how we weave together the many aspects of our identity. Hybridity helps name the ways that identity is a collage of gender, race, culture, age, region, class, ability, religion, language, and politics. How we hold these aspects together is shaped by the places we dwell and routes we travel. At any time in a place, particular aspects of our identity may come to the fore and become a lens through which we view the other aspects.

Self emerges from and in response to what place gathers.

Place gathers and presents to us the raw material for constructing our identity and vocation—we are the histories and relationships that place gathers. We take what place offers and weave it into who we are in ways that are creative, conformist, resistant, or a bit of all three. We can respond to what place presents us because we are conditioned but not determined by place. In the relationships gathered by place, we continually come into being and influence the becoming of others.

CAPACITIES OF THE SELF FOR PARTNERSHIP

Partnership is a key aspect of the way I discuss vocation and place. We partner with God's work in the world and we have a partnership with place.

God calls, and through place we are called into being and vocation. For some, the idea of partnership with God is theologically problematic because it seems to diminish God's sovereignty and fails to take seriously human fallenness. Sharing in work does not mean equality between co-workers—we follow God's lead in this partnership arrangement. In addition, *our* frailty and *our* limits do not limit the creativity of God to partner with us. The biblical witness is full of examples where God empowers and uses human vessels who are both gifted and broken to advance God's work in the world.

We can also point to several characteristics in the biblical witness that deepen our capacity to be in partnership with God and place. "Capacity for partnership" refers to the complexity and consistency of our partnership—not whether we can or cannot be in partnership with God at any point or condition in life. There are the various lists of spiritual gifts in the New Testament[2]—while individuals receive particular spiritual gifts, the intent is for the building of the body of Christ. There are the fruit of the Spirit found in Galatians 5:22-23.[3] While manifest in individuals, they are fruit shared collectively by those of faith. We might also think of the characteristics of those blessed in the Beatitudes of Matthew's Gospel (5:3-11): those poor in spirit, those who mourn, the meek, those who hunger and thirst for righteousness, those who exhibit mercy, the pure of heart, the peacemakers, those persecuted for righteousness sake, those being reviled on account of Jesus.

All of the prior characteristics are important, but I wish to bring attention to a trinity of capacities important to our partnership with God found in Paul's first letter to the Corinthians: *faith, hope, and love* (1 Cor 13:13). *Faith* provides trust, allowing us to follow God's lead, and an accrued confidence to take on the work of partnership with God. *Hope* supplies a longing that allows us to be resilient in the twists and turns of partnership with God. *Love*, the greatest in this trinity, gives us a capacity to transcend ourselves and to give ourselves for others.

Faith—Memory and the Unknown

Quite often we speak of faith as a willingness to leap into the unknown, as if we are spiritual daredevils. Such a framing tends to pit faith against reason—one has greater faith the more blind and unreasoned the leap. This framing also roots faith in the individual, even if faith originates beyond us as a gift from God. Additionally, this makes faith become ahistorical—one has greater faith if the leap defies the past. We should affirm that trust is at the heart of faith and trust draws on a range of rationalities, the faithfulness of God, *and memory*. Memory is particularly important here. Remembering and re-membering our personal and corporate past points to God's faithfulness and ways God acts in partnership with people and creation. The arc of that memory provides an accrued confidence about God and about us, which makes it possible to face the unknown.[4]

Hope—Resilience and Despair

Hope provides resiliency for the twists and turns of partnership with God, the contour of which can at times create frustration and despair. Hope helps us know that our partnership is not in vain. We experience hope when we consider the bigger picture of God's faithfulness throughout history and the promises of God leading forward. We experience hope when we see transformation in the particularity of persons and places. Whether considering our plight on a scale grand or granular, an attitude of thankfulness attunes us to signs of hope that fosters resiliency and eases despair.

Frustration and despair often raise questions of whether one should remain in particular places. Resiliency may help us continue our partnership with God in very challenging places and circumstances. However, being resilient does not mean that we are destined to stay in places and situations. Despite our best efforts in place-making, we need to move on to not suffer harm at the hand of dynamics we cannot change or control. As a church sign I saw once said, "We are called to be living sacrifices…not burnt offerings."[5] Even when things are going well, God may stir us to new places of growth and service. Sometimes the network of places in our daily lives must change to provide relief, balance, and freedom. Knowing when to shift from dwelling to moving is not easy. It is a matter of evaluating topophilia, cost to self, satisfaction, and the lure of the Spirit. When one cannot physically move, staying requires resiliency and setting boundaries to protect the self.[6]

Love—Self and the Other

Love gives us the capacity to transcend ourselves (to be more than merely our *selves*) and to live for others. This is not a matter of denouncing oneself or denigrating oneself. We must care for the gift of God's image in us so that we have a self to give to others, freely in love. If love truly casts out all fear[7] because nothing can separate us from God's love,[8] we have a liberating gift enabling us to be open to people and creation. That openness, that choice to love, often involves fear and pain as well as deep joy. Yet the freedom of love allows us to *have* fears and experience suffering without *being defined by* those fears and pains.[9] As we consider love as a capacity for partnership, we should mindful of care for place. Anthropocentrism limits love and worth to that which is human, and a primary dynamic of hate is to make others into something not human. Care for place interrupts that cycle, so that love opens us to all that place gathers whether human or not.

Three other capacities for partnership are important to add in light of my understanding of the self and place. These include integrity, agency, and mutuality. Each of these embodies an inherent tension in the interplay of self, place, and vocation. Integrity has a tension of continuity and change in the interaction between the self and place. Agency has a tension between interdependence and differentiation of the self with place. Mutuality has a tension between what individuals contribute to and receive from a place as it gathers them.

Integrity—Tension of Continuity and Change

In each experience of place, we must face questions about the integrity of our ongoing identity (continuity) and our openness to changes in that identity. God and place constantly call us into identity and vocation. Are we open to such evocation? Are we open to following a faith into the uncertain realm of the future? At the heart of this dilemma is clarity about the continuity of the forms/embodiments partnership takes and continuity of purpose in partnership. Conversations about vocation tend to focus on being true to one's authentic self. Too often, we emphasize continuity of form (being a pastor or leader) and lose sight of the purpose of our partnership with God in place (e.g., moving toward the Kin-dom of God). Ideally, we are constantly changing in form so that we remain the same (in purpose/commitment). Our authentic or true self is not a thing out there to find but a continuity of purpose alive across the many forms of our partnership with God. Of course, human proclivity to self-deception complicates our ability to assess the consistency between God's calling and what we embody. We need to avoid the two extremes of refusal to change and being in constant flux. Both interfere with our responsiveness to place and of God's calling via place. *The vibrant tension of continuity and change is a blend of offering the gifts of our historic selves for service to God's work in place and of receiving transformation by the work of God in place.*[10]

Agency—Tension between Interdependence and Differentiation

In each experience of place, we face questions about the ways we value our constitutive relationships—embracing and differentiating ourselves in the web of relationships in place. Place gathers that which constitutes us, but it does not determine us. We respond to what place gathers by deciding how we incorporate aspects of place into who we are. The extremes of over-identification with relationships (enmeshment) and of isolation from relationships (apathy) impede our agency (ability to effectively act and to create change). Enmeshment makes it difficult to be conscious of place—its dynamics, gifts, brokenness, and needs for transformation. Change involves disruption and often conflict. If we overly identify with our relationships, fears of losing relationships (i.e., ourselves) undercut our ability to foster constructive change. If we lack relationships and empathy, the lack of motivation and interest undercuts our agency for faithful change. *We must find the balance of interdependence and differentiation that creates empathy and agency to support our partnership with God.*

Mutuality—Tension between Contributing to and Receiving from Place

In each experience of place, we face questions of mutuality in our constitutive relationships—the flow of contributing to and receiving from relationships. In a culture preoccupied with the self, mutuality is often lost. Vocational understandings become concerned with what change an independent individual can create within a setting ("transformational leadership") and what an individual gains from a setting (experiences that boost one's resume).[11] We need honest awareness (humility) about the gifts and needs that we bring (our identity and vocational histories) to any particular place. Self-deception about these confuses our needs with the needs of place, which leads to manipulation that *takes* from place rather than *receiving* the gifts place offers. We risk being colonial rather than vocational. Mutuality is about gifts and blessings—shared graces, ecologies of graces, graces held in common. We offer our gifts and blessings, while at the same time opening ourselves to transformation from the gifts and blessing of place. In this mutuality, we encounter personal and social holiness. *We need to embrace a rhythm of giving and receiving from place that empowers others and ourselves in shared partnership with God.*

By highlighting the capacities above, I do not intend to devalue the many tools often used to discern individual vocation. My intent is to raise awareness about considerations that are often overlooked. We should consider these inputs for discerning vocation and leadership in the context of place: faith and spirituality, personality types, theological worldviews, psychological profiles, personal strengths, learning styles, leadership styles, family systems, and so on.

We often frame these capacities for partnership (integrity, agency, and mutuality) in relation to God and neighbor. We need to consider these capacities in relation to the ecological realm as well.

VOCATIONAL IMAGINATION, GRACE, AND AUTHOR-ING STORIES

Fostering capacities in individuals for partnership with *I Am—Place* involves formative discipleship and robust vocational imagination. Discipleship brings us into ever-deeper relationship with God through the study of scripture and tradition, along with worship, prayer, and service. Vocational imagination brings us into ever-deeper readiness for and responsiveness to the evocations of God and place. Narratives of lives in vocation fuel vocational imagination. Such narratives are unique to each person; no one has the same experiences, yet the patterns of the narratives found in them follow an oft-used plot drawn from one's community and place. Testimonies tend to describe a struggle building up to a pivotal period when God somehow comes through and renews hope, making a way out of no way. Faith journeys tend to depict the vicissitudes of trust and doubt in God in relation to life events and places, showing that God was with the person through it all. Call stories tend to move from sensing that God is addressing us to a period of denial to acceptance, ending with "Here I am, Lord." Vocational narratives connect our many instances of partnerships with God. This helps us recognize a pattern and trajectory in our ever-evolving identity and vocation.

Vocational narratives are essential to developing vocational imagination for at least three reasons. First, vocational narratives provide resources for forming identity. Second, narratives engage and shape our imagination (how we make connections between things) in ways informational and didactic instruction do not. They help us see and inhabit the world in particular ways. To do that we need to live into narratives—try out their views of the world and forms of partnership—rather than attempt to extract a list of how to be in vocation. In conjunction with practices, vocational narratives form us into traditions of faithful identity and partnership with God. Third, narratives can hold tensions in a generative way, without turning them into dichotomies needing resolution.[12] The tensions involved in capacities for partnership help animate the narratives of religious testimonies, faith journeys and call stories.

Stories and practices that foster rich vocational imagination mediate grace—grace in that they facilitate ways to redeem times of brokenness in our lives, they help us recognize and affirm giftedness, and they foster responsiveness to the evocation of God and place. A weakness, sin, or fault once taken as a deficit may become an asset (redeemed) for God's work and place. Rather than a private accomplishment on a resume, a skill or talent is a gift to contribute to *I Am—Place*. Faith and unconditional love make it possible to have fears without being those fears, which allows openness to the evocation of God and place. Redemptive and empowering stories and practices produce *graceful vocation*.

Living into stories with rich vocational imagination is a way of living into grace that revalues, reframes, and redeems life experiences and gifts. It is a graceful process exploring the claim "that all things work together for good for those who love God, who are called according to his purpose" (Rom 8:28). I do not believe that God causes tragedy. Nor do I believe that "redeeming" trauma takes away suffering or denies the evil at its source. God's creativity finds ways to redeem whatever it is possible to redeem. The question of Romans 8:28 becomes one of ends—what are we to do with tragedy, trauma, brokenness, and injustice so that we can be whole and responsive? Working out our salvation is more than redeeming the past and becoming whole. *All things* working together for good includes blessings as well as that which is broken, tragic, or sinful. This includes empowering and dedicating for God's use (sanctifying) our experiences, talents, gifts, and resources. Again, the question is one of ends—what are we to do with our experiences, talents, gifts, and resources? If the self is constructed by narratives, the grace-filled story lines offered by the Spirit, scripture, and faith community are in fact means for becoming new creations in Christ.[13] As new creations, both redeemed brokenness and empowered giftedness become integral to who we are. The Spirit creates us anew with freedom and power to dwell ever more deeply in our responsiveness to God and place—a holiness of engagement.

Story lines like these are available to us as resources in the traditions of place through the accumulated witness of the saints and favored stories of scripture. With each telling and retelling of experiences, individuals are *authoring* themselves through the resources of traditions and in turn, these traditions are *author-izing* individuals when personal narratives embody those flowing in the tradition. The authority of tradition is the power given them to author identity and vocation. A shadow side to this dynamic is when persons cannot see relevant story lines for them in their tradition and when communities *do not* authorize vocation. When there is a vocational disconnect between an individual and their tradition, is the individual a prophet in the midst of doubters, or is the individual a self-deceived person amidst truth-tellers? Such a situation holds issues of both injustice and faithful discernment.

The robustness of vocation among the members of a faith community is a function of the richness of vocational stories held and valued (authorized) in that community. We need to open the treasure chest of vocational stories available to us in our traditions and places. As we consider the vocational stories in the place of community, we must be critically conscious of the missing and muted stories. Their absence both curtails vocational imagination and delegitimizes some forms of vocation. We find vocational stories in the following:

- Historical saints of the church

- Everyday saints with us all the time (family, friends, mentors, brothers and sisters in Christ)

- Nonconformists who seem like anything but saints

- The cycles of life and habitat in creation

- Biblical heroes and heroines

- Denominational and congregational heroes and heroines

- Even secular saints (those we recognize as responding to love)

Essentially, we need to mindfully and critically dwell within the great cloud of witnesses. As we do so, we must know these witnesses in and through their love of place.

As we delve into narrative resources, the point is not so much imitation of exemplars, helpful as that may be. Nor is it a matter of accepting lofty standards of character seemingly beyond attainment. Rather, the goal is to resource vocational imagination. When we see a saint in a stained-glass window, we peer through them to the world and place we dwell. We do not create *ex nihilo*—we need resources from which to create. Engaging the cloud of witnesses that is tradition is akin to the gift of a Lego set. The box shows the item that the set makes, but children use those same building blocks to fashion something new after a few times of constructing that item. It is not unconstrained creativity, however—one is limited by the contents of the box.[14]

We delve into the cloud of witnesses when we

- Study scripture and tradition

- Hear witness and testimony[15]

- Participate in small groups

- Use educational approaches such as story-linking[16]

- Work in shared service

- Live in community

- Receive mentoring and discipleship

- Engage in worship, liturgical seasons, and holidays/feast days

- Honor memorials (these are deeply connected to place)

- Explore local histories and folklore

Leaders in communities of faith, particularly ordained persons, need to be mindful of the powerful implicit messages communicated by the ways they tell their own vocational stories. Too often, clergy call stories equate calling with ordained or professional ministry. Phrases such as "my call to ministry" (without qualifying the type of ministry) connote that ministry is a pastoral matter—all in the body of Christ are ministers, but not all are pastors. In addition, such phrases convey that the speaker was not in ministry or partnership with God prior to "receiving a call"—we are constantly being called by God. Apart from attending to the implicit messages, hearing pastoral call stories is best in the context of diverse lay, professional, and ordained call stories. This is not to minimize the significance of ordained ministry and leadership. Rather, it is taking seriously the power of such narratives to shape vocational imagination.

SUMMARY

The perspectives that influence a rethinking of vocation and of place also influence my view of the self—God calls in each moment of experience, creation is in process, and we emerge from relationships gathered by place. More specifically, this chapter presented these claims about the self:

- The self is a process, the continuity of individual moments of experience.

- The nature of human experience is narrative.

- Identity is a matter of belonging.

- The self is hybrid.

- Self emerges from and in response to what place gathers.

One of the correctives to our understandings of vocation I presented in chapter 3 is rooting vocation in place and not solely in the individual. Doing so does not diminish the importance of individual identity in vocation. Persons utilize significant capacities for partnership with God:

- Faith that connects memory of the past and openness to the unknown

- Hope that navigates resilience and despair

- Love that bridges self and the Other

- Integrity that holds the tension of continuity and change

- Agency that maintains interdependence and differentiation

- Mutuality that balances contributing to and receiving from place

These capacities as part of one's identity and vocational imagination depend on the resources in the traditions of place. In terms of Christianity, this means the accumulated witness of the saints and scripture. The richness of vocational imagination in a faith community flows from the richness of vocational stories held and valued in that community.

At this point, we have addressed four key components in the vocational mix—understandings of God's work in the world,[17] the nature of vocation, the nature of place, and the nature of self. In sum,

- God's work involves *gathering and forming the world* in light of the Kin-dom of God.

- Vocation is a *process of partnership* with God's work in and for the world within and *evoked by particular places.*

- Place is a *particular gathering of formative relationships*—a process of gathering groups of people, creatures, plants, climate, and physical structures into a web of relationships—not just a location on a map.

The self emerges in response to God from the relationships of place. Narratives give a sense of continuity to the many aspects of identity and many experiences over time.

With these components of vocational imagination in mind, the next three chapters present aspects of engaging in vocational theology. Chapter 6 addresses vocational praxis in attending to the places we dwell. Chapter 7 engages vocational praxis in relation to the routes we travel. Chapter 8 considers implications of a vocation-in-place perspective for practical theology and for fostering vocation-in-place within congregations.

FOR REFLECTION

Personal Perspective

1. Describe a place and time when you felt authentic—truly you—and felt like your whole self showed up. What about that place and what it gathered helped make that happen?

2. Think of the various places and routes of your life. What are significant places shaping your identity? How and why did they shape who you are?

3. What assumptions about the self in relation to place in this chapter do you find useful or challenging?

4. What stories do you tell about yourself and how do these create your sense of self and identity?

5. In what ways do you see your identity as "hybrid?"

6. In which capacities for partnership do you have depth and/or need development?

7. The list of capacities for partnership in this chapter is not exhaustive. What capacities do you think are important to add? Why?

8. What have you learned about yourself and your capacities for partnership through conversations with mentors and various inventories (e.g. spiritual gifts, personality types, strength finder, learning styles)?

9. What stories of other people in your life and faith community do you draw upon for inspiration and forming your own identity? How did these persons embody vocation and engage place?

Leadership Perspective

10. In what places where you lead do you feel most and least yourself? What about those places and what is gathered help create those experiences?

11. How are you helping persons to think theologically about their identity... to be practical everyday theologians?

12. In addition to rites of confirmation and commissioning, what are ways you foster a congregational culture that is continually confirming and commissioning people (explicitly and implicitly) into vocation, service, and ministry?

13. How do you curate and make available a rich range of stories from which persons can draw to craft their identities and vocation?

Congregational Perspective

14. Where and how frequently are persons given the opportunity to tell their story...to practice authoring themselves as disciples and as partners with God?

15. What stories are authorized and suppressed in this congregation? Who are lifted up as saints (exemplary disciples and partners with God) and who is not? Why?

16. In addition to the rite of confirmation, what are ways the congregation is continually confirming and commissioning people (explicitly and implicitly) into vocation, service, and ministry?

17. Describe the range of stories in the congregation from which persons can draw to craft their identities and vocation.

Chapter 6
ATTENDING TO ROOTS: VOCATION AND THE PLACES WE DWELL

HOW LONG, O LORD?

The question ran through my mind over and over on the way back to our office in Plant 18: *How long, O Lord, how long?* It was like so many meetings before. My product development team went to the pilot production facility across town for a project update. The development team I led included four engineers from different departments. The pilot facility was a separate organization in the division. It was where our company developed the production processes for our new auto parts before sending them to a non-union plant in Mexico. The manufacturing liaison at the facility for our project was difficult to work with. Once again, it felt like the liaison's mantra during the meeting had been how everything about the project was messed up: the design was bad, the assembly processes were new, the timeline was unrealistic, there were not enough resources, and so on. I was sure others on my team felt beaten down again. I tried to keep in mind that the liaison was in a high-pressure job where he had to fix many problems with little time and few resources. A lot of crud rolled down the organization into his office. It probably did not help that he was a seasoned veteran of manufacturing and I was a relatively new engineer. Plus, there just seemed to be an inherent friction in the organization between the ivory tower product engineers and the real-world manufacturing engineers.

Once back at my desk, I stewed and pondered. Our office was an open second-floor space packed with desks without cubicle dividers to offer any private space. I could see the demeanor of the team. In this place, I worked hard to practice what I was learning about faith, education, and community from seminary and about group dynamics and organizational development from corporate trainings. I tried to create a team that was effective, creative, and productive. I also tried to create a team whose relationships fostered respect, collaboration, support, self-worth, and personal growth. When at the pilot facility, I tried to facilitate meetings with the same intent as for my team. The liaison and I were playing by two different rules of engagement. I looked out the window at the vast complex of manufacturing plants across the street. Was I naively trying to fashion a kind of place alien to the realities on those production floors across the street? Why was it taking so long for God to show me the way out of here? I really wanted to say, "I'm out of here…now."

This chapter offers a vocational praxis for attending to the places in which we dwell. If place evokes vocation, then reflectively engaging place is essential to vocational discernment. We will begin with perspectives and attitudes toward the idea of dwelling. Next, we will develop five movements in a vocation-in-place praxis that explore our connections with place, raise awareness of the gathering of relationships in place, and claim our partnerships with God in place. I think beginning this praxis with the affective dimensions of our connectedness with place is important for at least two reasons. For one, it acknowledges the underlying reality of our connectedness and how ranges of feelings (positive and negative) frame that connectedness. For another, emotional dimensions of connectedness shape our motivations, actions, resiliency, and commitments. Places and their dynamics are not abstract problems to fix.

The following vocation-in-place praxis relates to the places of the pilot production facility and the engineering office. These places created a range of emotions—conflict, frustration, defensiveness, confusion. I longed to leave, but that was not happening any time soon. These places gathered me with a particular set of people, relationships, ethos, and physical environments. I could recognize dynamics that helped and hindered flourishing of life and the Spirit. Over time, I began to realize that my team's office was a place of calling simply because that was where I was. Whether God intended me to be there and whether God wanted me to stay were separate questions. My imagination of God's concern for relationships shaped how I responded to the call of God-in-place. Yes, my team's office was a place that evoked calling—so too was the pilot production facility, and my home, community, seminary, and church. They were each places I showed up in and encountered God-in-place.

DWELLING IN PLACES

In addition to asking what on earth God is doing, being in partnership with God also involves asking *where on earth are we?* Knowing where we are and the nature of our places is very important for recognizing how God-in-place calls us into being and into vocation. This task involves considering our attitudes about place, our presence in place, and an approach for attending to place.

Experiences and Attitudes about Place

Our experiences and attitudes about place profoundly shape the ways we dwell in place. Given that we always exist *some* place, the issue is not whether we dwell in a place but rather the nature of that dwelling. Three initial attitudes about places warrant attention.

One attitude is a pejorative view of dwelling in place. For many persons, dwelling has the negative connotations of narrowness and stuck-ness. When someone *dwells* on a topic, it becomes a singular exclusionary focus. Such dwelling is irritating, particularly when the focus is a fault or mistake on our part. Within a culture that values change and movement—and falsely assumes everyone has freedom to move—dwelling also has pejorative connotations of being parochial and static. When we think of creatures in their habitat, we do not think of their dwelling as some form of arrested development. Why should we think less of ourselves when we dwell in the places of our lives? When associated with places deemed threatening or impoverished, people are pejoratively labeled (e.g., ghetto dweller, swamp-dweller), which makes dwelling a matter of social class or character.

In light of the ways I have presented place as dynamic and open, parochial and static notions of dwelling should not hold. Place is a continual process of gathering particular sets of people, creatures, plants, climate, and physical structures—it is the unfolding web of relationships between God, humans, and creation. Shaped by culture and practices, "place" is the way we imagine this localized web and our position in it—our relational way of being in the world. Habits in the process of forming relationships between elements give places their character. Places are full of assets, hindrances, and graces for flourishing.

A second attitude is obliviousness to place. Some persons are not very conscious of place or are conscious of only narrow aspects of place. This might be due to the high demands of economic, physical, and emotional survival, or a hectic lifestyle. Disconnectedness with place may arise from having power that provides one with independence from circumstances. Obliviousness might also stem from being so caught up in one's own vision of a place that it overruns and colonizes a place. This last point can make place an abstraction to analyze, a problem to solve, or a set of needs awaiting a ministry. Such attitudes easily form relationships with place that are condescending, motivated to relieve feelings of guilt, and colonial.

A third attitude is rejection of places. Many persons are keenly aware of the place they dwell and live in resistance to that place. It may be that a place for a variety of reasons does not suit one's preferences and values. A place may lack what one needs to pursue hopes, desires, and personal flourishing. Places may be so damaging and oppressive that they cannot be embraced—they must be resisted and rejected.

Dwelling and Presence

Dwelling involves participating in the relational gathering and meaning-making processes that transform space into place. Recognizing what place gathers about us, experiencing relationships among the gathered, and finding meaning in these relationships requires one's *attentiveness*, an engaged mindfulness that allows us to be aware and intentional, receptive and resilient, and to personally, socially, physically, ecologically, and spiritually show up.

As we become intentional about dwelling and place evoking us, we face a very pragmatic question about the scope of our attentiveness. Where am I present? Where are the edges of the places I dwell? Unlike boundaries on a political map, places do not have well-defined edges. We become aware that we are in a different place because where we are creates a different feeling in us. Pinpointing that change in feeling is often not possible.[1] For example, the city of Delaware is just north of Columbus, Ohio, and suburban growth increasingly connects them. It is hard to know where the edges of Delaware and Columbus *as places* (not municipalities) exist. In some sense, the places of Delaware and Columbus are overlapping, but in another sense a hybrid place of its own exists between them. Places also nest within each other—our dwelling is a mosaic of particular places. The particular places we live (e.g., home, work, school, church[2]) are nested in larger communities, counties, and states, which themselves exist in ecological regions and watersheds—all of this ultimately residing within *I Am—Place*.

Within this network, our mode of dwelling in place constantly shifts. Changing locations is naturally one cause for shifting modes of dwelling. Perhaps more important is the impact of our awareness and intentionality about place and dwelling. Awareness and intentionality bring depth to dwelling in a particular locale, and they bring breadth to dwelling within larger spheres of places. For example, awareness and intentionality in the place of home bring to the fore the presence or lack of care, nurture, shelter, safety, and sustenance. Awareness and intentionality also connect the ways we dwell at home with the dynamics of the natural and built environment, community, region, and ultimately the divine.

If dwelling involves showing up, then we need to ask *where* we spend time, *how* we spend time there, and *why* we spend time there (as opposed to other places).

An Approach for Attending to Places We Dwell and Vocations Evoked

If place evokes vocation, then attending to place becomes integral to vocational discernment. Such discernment involves the following:

- Attending to our connections with place by asking, "How is this place claiming me and how do I *belong* (or not)?"

- Attending to the gathering of place by asking, "What and who is gathered in this place?"

- Attending to our identity and vocational narratives by asking, "How is this place gathering me?"

- Attending to grace and brokenness by asking, "What relationships emerge in this place and how do they foster and hinder flourishing of life and Spirit?"

- Attending to our role in forming relationships by asking, "How am I to be in partnership with God's place-making work?"

The remainder of this chapter describes these movements in attending to place and vocations that place evokes.

HOW IS THIS PLACE CLAIMING ME AND HOW DO I BELONG (OR NOT)?

The ways that a place claims one vary widely. Place may claim us through memories, commitments, duties, principles, relationships, possibilities, and hopes. Place may claim us through habits, constraints, coercion, and lack of alternatives. Knowing places does not necessarily mean that we feel connected with them. Lacking such connection, places and movement between them lose their power to call us into vocation. We need to consider the webs of emotional dynamics shaping our motivations, actions, resilience, and commitment relative to both place and God-in-place. These emotional dynamics emerge in the tensions of belonging and alienation, being claimed and rejected, solidarity and indifference, empathy and numbness, agency and powerlessness. The following sections explore these tensions.

Belonging ←→ Alienation

The root of the word *belong* connotes "being very appropriate to" and the "long" in be*long* suggests "a desire for."[3] So, belonging combines a pragmatic and emotional sense of being in the right place—a recognition on my part and that of others that this is *my place*; these are *my people*. In contrast to belonging, the dynamics of place can designate people, creatures, and plants as *out of place*, that is, *alien*. In terms of people, this is a process of othering, objectification, and alienation—putting people out. In terms of creatures and plants, this is a debate about what is native and what is invasive.

Claimed ←→ Rejected

Belonging brings with it a sense of being claimed by place. When place claims us, we recognize we are not our own. The point is not conforming but rather contributing and being faithful to the fullness of our relationships in place. Such commitments to those gathered by place circumscribe our freedom. Alienation brings with it a sense of being rejected by place. When a place rejects us or we close ourselves to being claimed, we are doubly diminished—we lose access to resources for our flourishing and the contributions of our talents languish.

Solidarity ←→ Indifference

Solidarity involves an identification with others in place and is rooted in a recognition of shared cause or common plight. It is a connectedness of purpose that may or may not have a strong emotional component—even if one does not particularly like others, one can be in solidarity with them. In contrast, indifference arises when we see little or no shared pursuit, and when coupled with emotional disinterest, any sense of connectedness fades.

Empathy ↔ Numbness

Empathy is identification with the experiences and situations of others. It has distinct emotional and existential dimensions. Whereas solidarity is a connectedness of purpose, empathy is an experiential connectedness that may or may not be connected to common cause. Think of the empathy reflected in the story of the Good Samaritan. Empathy involves sharing a wide range of emotions and experiences ranging from joy to suffering. If we attend to only positive emotional connections, we may simply be nice; if we attend to only to negative emotional connections, we may simply engage in pity. In contrast to empathy, emotional numbness arises when we fail to connect with another. Death of emotional connectedness with others not only objectifies others; it signals a degree of death in our own humanity. Numbness obstructs not only compassion, but also the anger and indignation that can fuel action to change the situations that create suffering.

Agency ↔ Powerlessness

Every place involves dynamics of power because power points to one's ability to influence others and environment. We can also describe this as a terrain of agency. Differences in gifts, resources, roles, relationships, and abilities shape the power terrain. The degree to which the terrain of power leads to agency or oppression depends a great deal on the explicit and implicit role of domination, bias, and obliviousness in a place. Agency is the ability to respond with integrity and dignity to the dynamics of our personal history and the place we dwell. Agency makes a difference in the nature of self and place, whether the magnitude of that difference is small or large. Oppression and habituation to our past can cause us to lose sight of agency, leading to a sense of powerlessness and helplessness.

Our sense of connectedness plays a significant role in our sense of vocation and place. When the majority of categories for understanding our connectedness with place are positive, we are likely to delve more deeply into our partnership with God in that place. When the opposite is true, we tend to question, with good reason, whether God is calling us in a particular place.[4] Our connectedness shapes how we discern whether partnership with God and engagement with place are worth the cost.

ATTENDING QUESTIONS

1. What are my experiences in this place relative to the categories of belonging, being claimed, solidarity, empathy and agency? Use the chart to guide your thinking.

	Degree that I experience (either/both)	How I experience	Source of experience
Belonging and alienation			
Being claimed and rejected			
Solidarity with and indifference to others			
Empathy and emotional numbness toward others			
Agency and powerlessness			

2. To what extent is the combined experience across these categories positive? How does this provide joy and draw you more deeply into place and partnership with God there?

3. To what extent is the combined experience across these categories negative? How does this shape your view of vocation and place?

4. How do the webs of emotional dynamics relative to both place and God-in-place influence your motivations, actions, satisfaction, resilience, and resolve for vocation in this place?

WHAT AND WHO ARE GATHERED IN THIS PLACE?

This is an overwhelming question! A place gathers so many diverse things, and more often than not we are oblivious to them. Perhaps we are inattentive or preoccupied with self or survival. Perhaps we are subject to the hazards of familiarity. Perhaps we are in denial. Perhaps we are embedded in privilege or suffer oppression. Attending to what is gathered involves stepping back and taking a fresh look through consciousness-raising questions, aided by place-related tools and methodologies. It is important that this be a process focused on naming and identifying. We must know what is present before we can value it, recognize relationships between what is present, and analyze the consequences of those relationships.

Gathered by and in Place

Places gather all the raw material of the relationships that make us who we are. It is part of the power of place to evoke us into existence and vocation. The lens of gathering focuses on knowing the places we dwell and our movements between places. This is both a prayerful and a studied knowing. Prayerful, in that we focus our attention[5] on the activity of the Spirit, signs of the Kin-dom, graces embodied, and brokenness displayed. Studied, in that we draw upon diverse tools to recognize the many personal, social, and ecological layers of place. Through prayer and study, we not only know place but also begin the process of valuing and transforming it.

We attend to the gathering of place in different ways. We learn a great deal about what place gathers by simply awakening and focusing our attention and our senses. Basic questions can prompt such attentiveness and the practice of using them fosters habits of mind, a way of seeing the world, a form of mindfulness, presence, and spirituality. Questions prompting attentiveness also serve to prompt research to help us know more fully and deeply. They lead us to tools such as demographic, political, and ecological maps and ethnography. These tools expand our sense of place and address ways we are oblivious to places. Engagement of place is analogous to engaging a sacred text. We can know a great deal by close reading and being guided by interrogative questions, but we also draw upon biblical study tools to read even more closely.

We attend to the gathering of place with varying breadth of scope. The broadest scope to consider is the place we dwell as a whole. The narrowest scope might be aspects of our home, office, classroom, or place of worship. Between these extremes are all the particular places nested within the place we dwell—neighborhoods, communities, and regions.

We attend to the gathering of place through several frames of reference. Using multiple frames helps us pay attention. We look for the peoples, creatures, plants, natural environments, built environments, sociocultural dimensions, and embodiment in place.

ATTENDING QUESTIONS

For the various levels of place, we attend to what is gathered by addressing these questions through observation and research:

Peoples

1. Who is present and where? Consider characteristics such as race and ethnicities, countries of origin, gender, sexual orientation and identity, age, persons with disabilities, economic class, religion, and politics.

2. Who is *not* present?

3. Who is seemingly invisible and to whom?

Creatures

4. What creatures (domestic, wild, agricultural) are present? This question is relevant even in dense urban settings with little green space.

Plants

5. What plants are present indoors and outside (pots, atria, gardens, landscapes, greenspaces, agriculture)?

Natural environment/habitat(s)

6. What is the prevailing weather over time and seasons (climate)? (temperatures, precipitation, winds, humidity, cloud cover)

7. What natural resources are present and where? What is their quality? (water, air, land/soil, energy, materials)

8. What natural habitats/ecosystems are present? (wetlands, prairies/meadows, streams, lakes/reservoirs, woodlands, mountains)

Built environment/habitat (human products)

9. What art, images, graphics, or icons are present in displays, galleries, advertisements, and signs?

10. What memorials and 2structures prompting memory are present?

11. What kinds of buildings are present (houses, condos, apartments, offices, stores, restaurants, libraries, community centers, religious buildings, government buildings, recreation facilities, entertainment venues)?

12. Where is humanly produced waste and pollution handled, transported, and deposited?

13. Where do persons obtain food and water?

14. What means of transportation (car, bus, rail, subway, plane, foot, bike, watercraft) and their related infrastructure (roads, tracks, tunnels, airport, walkways, lanes/paths, waterways) are present?

Sociocultural structures

15. What cultures, subcultures, and overall ethos exist?

16. What histories, memories, and narratives are present?

17. What marks time, seasons, and the rhythm of life?

18. Where are sacred places?

19. What social institutions are present?

20. What music permeates the place?

21. What practices shape this place?

Embodiment

22. How do you encounter this place through the senses (sight, smell, taste, touch, sound)?

HOW IS THIS PLACE GATHERING ME?

Our sense of identity and vocation emerges from our current relationships and from personal history. Place gathers these sources of identity and vocation; thus, place gathers me in two ways. One is that our sense of self emerges from and in response to what a particular place gathers relationally. This brings attention to the resources place gathers for constructing our identity and vocation in the present. As we form relationships with what is in place, we form our self and vocation. We take what place offers and weave it into who we are in ways that are oppositional, conformist, or a bit of both. In the midst of the relationships gathered by place, we continually come into being and contribute to the becoming of others.

A second way is that our sense of self emerges from how place gathers past experiences and partnerships with God temporally. We bring a great deal with us as we enter a place: memories, knowledge, skills, dispositions, gifts, graces, wounds, and personalities. People often think of these as packaged into pre-formed identity and vocation that one contextualizes for a particular place. However, if vocation and identity are not "things" but processes, then we need to think of what we bring into a place as being alongside all of the resources that place gathers for identity, vocation, and relationships. As what we have been interacts with the web of relationships in place, with *I Am—Place*, we fashion a personal history, a self-understanding, a sense of connection with place. Identity and vocational narratives hold together the experiences in our personal history. These narratives mark the trajectory of gifts and brokenness we bring to places. The self-we-have-been and the self-we-are-becoming in a particular place may have great continuity, great discontinuity, or more likely a creative mix. At the intersection of the self-we-have-been and place, the stories of who we are become recreated in ways that replicate the past and make us open to God's creative call.

ATTENDING QUESTIONS

Relationally Gathering Me in the Present

1. How do I spend time and why do I spend time in this place?

2. What personal, social, and cultural aspects of myself are emphasized and valued?

3. To what extent do I feel freedom, belonging, and empowerment?

4. What personal, social, and cultural aspects of myself are minimized and undervalued?

5. To what extent do I feel constrained, rejected, and discounted?

6. What expectations and roles do I accept and reject in this place?

7. Who am I in this place and to what extent does this feel authentic?

Temporally Gathering My Past in the Present

8. How is this place similar to or resonant with prior places in my life?

9. How is this place different from prior places in my life?

10. What does this place stir up from my past, whether positive or negative?

11. What resources, gifts, and graces do I bring to this place?

12. What needs, challenges, and brokenness do I bring to this place?

13. How does this place fit into the arc of my life journey (past, present, future)?

Engaging the questions of how place gathers my history also requires inner work and reflection to consider the legacy and trajectory of one's past. We engage in this when we construct a resume[6] or complete a job application. This is where many of the inventories used for self-awareness enter. These include Myers-Briggs personality types, spiritual gifts, leadership styles, conflict styles, theological worlds, StrengthsFinder, MMPI (Minnesota Multiphasic Personality Inventory), learning styles, multiple intelligences, and Intercultural Development Inventory, among others. Nominating committees and ordination committees play a role in this process of discerning the gifts and graces we bring to place as well.

WHAT RELATIONSHIPS EMERGE IN THIS PLACE AND HOW DO THEY INFLUENCE FLOURISHING OF LIFE AND THE SPIRIT?

The questions about what place gathers and our connectedness with place are descriptive in nature. In turning our attention to relationships between what place gathers, we become more evaluative. How does the nature of all the relationships in place help or hinder the flourishing of life and the Spirit? Where are grace and brokenness? The discernment of our responsive partnership with God-in-place depends greatly on the answer to these questions.

Our evaluation of relationships in place must involve *humility*—a combination of trust in what we know in our bones, attention to the hazards of self-deception, and awareness of our ignorance about what is going on in our place(s). We also need to integrate both appreciation and critique of relationships in our evaluations—awareness of blessings and graces (assets) along with awareness of problems and needs. Appreciation of giftedness is an important resource for mutuality, transformation, resiliency, vitality, flourishing, faithfulness and holding at bay the tendencies to rescue, patronize, and pity others.

Relationships are complex—they have many dimensions and facets, so no single perspective is complete. Relationships are dynamic and changing. Thinking in terms of place provides an opportunity for intentionally addressing the complexity of relationships. We have a workable ground for considering brokenness and flourishing of life and the Spirit in social, interpersonal, personal, and ecological ways. In each of these spheres we practice spiritual as well as ethical discernment because in each we encounter God's concern for the world. Brokenness and flourishing are matters of sin and grace.

We experience the relationships in place through structures of society, culture, and power. Systems such as racism, sexism, classism, anthropocentrism, heterosexism, and ableism often distort the terrain of relationships. The connections between these individual systems complicate the understanding of this terrain. The lens of intersectionality brings the relational terrain of place into focus, or more accurately, brings out what hidden dynamics there may be. We will need practices that open up intersections of relationships (human and ecological) for transformation: hearing into voice,[7] seeing into visibility,[8] and crossing borders into understanding.

Social Brokenness ⟷ Social Flourishing

On one level, we experience the relationships in place through structures of society, culture, and power. How do sociocultural systems help and hinder flourishing of life and the Spirit? They hinder flourishing of life and the Spirit when systems such as racism, sexism, classism, anthropocentrism, heterosexism, and ableism, along with their intersections, break relationships and dehumanize. Dehumanizing turns the neighbor into an *alien other* and, once other-ed, opens the neighbor to ill-treatment in a variety of ways. In some places, we may consciously or unconsciously benefit from one or more of these systems and be oblivious to how such systems fracture communities, others, and ourselves. For example, I benefit from white privilege when as a white male I do not need to worry about having someone call the police just because I am walking in the neighborhood. I do not seek out this privilege nor am I very conscious of it because it seems normal. In contrast, a white woman may walk in the same neighborhood and share my freedom from worry about police but instead be worried about being assaulted. Social conditions break relationships by pitting one group against another. For example, groups sharing the experience of unemployment and poverty may be at odds with others because of differing causes (such as closing of businesses, forms of discrimination, and systemically poor education) for their struggles.

Social and cultural systems can also be beneficial by providing for everyone the prerequisites for flourishing in the Spirit. This begins with addressing physical needs of food, shelter, and safety in just and sustainable ways. However, survival is not flourishing, nor the biblical witness for fullness of life. Social and cultural systems promote flourishing when they embody such things as care, respect, tolerance, justice, resiliency, creativity, and empowerment.

We need only remember God's concern for the poor, the widow, and the alien and Jesus's restoration of people to community to recognize the spiritual grounding of social relationships.

Interpersonal Brokenness ⟷ Interpersonal Flourishing

When we engage other persons and creation, we do so in particular concrete ways. Our personal relationships will, to varying degrees, both reflect and challenge prevailing sociocultural and ecological systems. A native speaker of English may relate to a native speaker of Spanish nationalistically as an "illegal" or as a neighbor with a Spanish heritage. Below social systems, the particularity of interpersonal relationships brings to the fore dynamics of personality, individual histories, shared experiences,

113

conflicts, common hopes, habits, and tastes. Friends, foes, families, and strangers are a blend of such things.

Interpersonal dynamics hinder flourishing of life and the Spirit when they break interpersonal relationships through specific acts of emotional and physical harm. The personal aspect of such harm can easily lead recipients of harm to question themselves—*What did I do to cause or deserve this?* Shame, loss of self-worth, and even loss of personhood can result.

In contrast, interpersonal dynamics help flourishing of life and the Spirit when we love and are loved; when we offer and receive grace; when we are heard and when we hear another; when we are seen and when we see others. They flourish when we give ourselves to each other. Love and grace are not just matters of emotional intimacy. Love and grace at their roots are matters of being taken seriously—that our existence makes a difference to others and to God.

We need only remember in the Great Commandment—love of neighbor is second only to love of God—to recognize the spiritual grounding of interpersonal relationships. In the face of another we see the image of God, and in creation we see the reflection of God.

Personal Brokenness ←→ Personal Flourishing

We may be graced and broken by others socially and interpersonally. Intrapersonally, we engage the inner relationships of our personal history in place with graces and brokenness of our own making. How do intrapersonal dynamics help and hinder flourishing of life and the Spirit? We struggle to flourish when we remain habituated to disabling coping strategies and self-understandings; when we break ourselves by accepting and internalizing the violence of others against us; when we break ourselves by allowing ourselves to perpetuate harm against others; when we reject the gifts of love and grace offered by God.

We flourish by embracing the ways God offers us love, grace, hope, and purpose in the moment and for the future—offers us new ways of being whole as we honor the image of God in us, steward our blessings, and redeem the brokenness of experiences in each place of life. Grace and creativity allow us to dwell in place without being determined by place. Dr.

James Earl Massey explained this dynamic once in relation to the Sermon on the Mount (Matt 5:39-42). When Jesus says to turn the other cheek, to give your shirt when someone takes your coat, and to go a second mile when forced to go a mile, he is teaching agency and resiliency. In these examples, going beyond the demand turns the tables. Rather than be determined by the demand, one responds with the agency of choice among limited options.

We need only remember that we are made in the image of God and the unconditional love of God for us to recognize the spiritual grounding of our inner lives.

Ecological Brokenness ←→ Ecological Flourishing

Thinking in terms of place pushes us to evaluate our relationships with the rest of creation as part of our partnership with God in place. How do ecological dynamics help and hinder flourishing of all life and the Spirit? Human activity hinders ecological flourishing in many ways: unsustainable consumption, pollution, global warming, mismanagement of resources, and arrogance about understanding of ecosystems. Our ecological interdependence means that the harm we do to ecosystems harms humans in turn. The consequences are particularly significant for marginalized peoples who often dwell in areas of higher pollution, hazardous manufacturing and chemical use, and natural resource extraction (mining, drilling, deforestation, etc.). Ecological harm also breaks the trust and relationships between generations of humans and between humans and creatures. In this regard, the sins of parents do fall upon their children.

Creation flourishes with a basic orientation of gratitude and respect for the grace that is the web of relationships making life even possible. Gratitude reminds us that ultimately we cannot create what we need to survive and thrive—creation is a gift of God. Respect reminds us that creation is more than humanity and we are just a part of a web of life. The intricacy of human and ecological relationships means there is not fullness of life without both human and ecological flourishing. We might say the Great Commandment to love God and neighbor implicitly involves love of creation. As we care for the gathering of

115

the Spirit, humans, and creation that is place, we live into this Great Commandment.

We need only remember that God the creator deemed the universe good and where brokenness exists, creation groans for redemption (Rom 8:22) to recognize the spiritual grounding of ecological relationships.

ATTENDING QUESTIONS

1. In what ways do I recognize or experience brokenness in this place?

	Signs of brokenness	Causes for brokenness
Social		
Interpersonal		
Intrapersonal		
Ecological		

2. In what ways do I recognize or experience flourishing in this place?

	Signs of flourishing	Sources of flourishing
Social		
Interpersonal		
Intrapersonal		
Ecological		

3. What graces and assets for flourishing of life and the Spirit are present in this place?

	Signs of grace	Assets/resources for flourishing
Social		
Interpersonal		
Intrapersonal		
Ecological		

PLACEMAKING: HOW AM I TO BE IN PARTNERSHIP WITH GOD IN THIS PLACE?

God is relational, and God's work in the world is very much about forging right relationships. In Genesis, we read that God creates a universe that is diverse and interrelated. The Great Commission (Matt 28:18-20) points to God reconciling the world unto God's self. The Great Commandment (Matt 22:35-39) involves God fostering in us love for neighbors. The formation of Israel told in the Hebrew Bible and emergence of the church as the body of Christ in the New Testament reveal God's desire for communal ways of being human. Micah 6:8 emphasizes God's work to create a world of peaceable and just relationships. The parable of final judgement in Matthew 25 reflects God's care for the suffering and marginalized in the world.

Given the witness to God's attention to relationships and our creation in God's image as relational and interdependent, it seems impossible that our vocations would not also be about attending to relationships. In light of the overwhelmingly vast web of human and nonhuman relationships, we might ask *which* relationships make a vocational claim on us. Such a question is much like the one asked of Jesus that prompted the telling of the parable of the Good Samaritan (Luke 10:25-27)—"Who is my neighbor?" At the end of the parable, Jesus asks who "was a neighbor to the man who fell into the hands of robbers?" To be a neighbor requires being in a shared place. The Samaritan entered the place of the injured traveler and became neighbor through empathy and care-giving. Pragmatically, a relatively small number of relationships significantly sway us. Place is the gathering of those concrete mutual relationships that influence us and that we can influence, the relationships in which it is possible to be a neighbor.

God (*I Am—Place*) is the place of all gathering—God is all about gathering. As creator, God gathered formlessness into stars, sky, land, seas, vegetation, animals, and humans. God gathered tribes, wanderers, slaves, and aliens into a people. As redeemer, God gathers brokenness and blessing into personal, social, and ecological wholeness. As sustainer, God continues to gather people and creation into the unfolding Kin-dom of God. God's holiness is wrapped up in God's ability to gather everything for the glory of God and the good of all creation. In every moment of experience, God is offering a way for persons and communities to gather their past into a meaningful purpose. From this perspective, gathering is a work of redemptive and empowering grace. If we are to be in partnership with God in attending to relationships, we must also take part in God's work of gathering and being gathered. In the absence of gathering, in the absence of place, what relationships exist for attending to? This should seem obvious, but we often thwart gathering. At times, zeal for purity rather than holiness leads to active efforts to purge and dis-place rather than gather. At other times, self-deception about our hospitableness creates an indifference to gathering. In some cases, desire for control distorts gathering into conquest of others.

Our evaluation of relationships in place also needs to consider our situation in a place. We need to assess the ways we are

- *Subject* to the consequences of sin and grace in place

- *Complicit* in the patterns of sin and grace in place

- *Agents* in creating patterns of sin and grace in place

Awareness of our involvement in the graces and brokenness of place balances personal, social, and ecological holiness. Sometimes transformation of place involves change in circumstances—sometimes we change the circumstances through change in ourselves.

Place-making is a response to tend the gifts and brokenness of place in light of God's work in the world, the unfolding of the Kin-dom of God. Tending to place means fostering a gratitude that manifests and nurtures the graces woven into places by God. Tending to place means participating in continual valuing, revaluing, and re-forming of relationships toward flourishing—that is, sharing in redeeming work. Being equipped for place-making draws deeply on our formation as disciples of Jesus: knowing scripture and our heritage, fruits of the Spirit, spirituality, prayer, worship, community, and servanthood. Place-making also requires a commitment to our own transformation as we encounter the relationships of place and expand our responsiveness to vocation—in essence, our deepening sanctification. In place-making, we practice both the Great Commandment and the Great Commission as dimensions of the Kin-dom of God.

As we continually form the relationships in a place, we engage in *place-making*. The key vocational,[9] spiritual, and ethical questions are whether our place-making is a faithful response to the call of God-in-place (*I Am—Place*). Does our place-making reflect God's desire for the nature of relationships between God and people, God and creation, self and neighbor, and humans and creation? Is our forming of personal, social, spiritual, and ecological relationships in place consistent with what we believe God is doing in the world? How we answer these questions about our place-making depends a lot on our location within Christian tradition, but it seems these common relational themes shape Christian imaginations about faithful place-making:

- Relationships honor the image and reflection of God in human and nonhuman creation. (*Creation*, Gen 1:1–2:4)

- Relationships bear the marks of justice, kindness, and humility. (*What the Lord Requires*, Mic 6:8)

- Relationships reflect love of God and love of neighbor as two facets of the same love. (*The Great Commandment*, Matt 22:35-39)

- Relationships reflect the life and way of Jesus.[10] (*The Great Commission*, Matt 28:18-20)

- Relationships embody self-giving love for one another. (*A New Com-*

mandment, John 13:34)

- Relationships show particular responsiveness to those suffering and marginalized. (*Care for the Least,* Matt 25:31-46)

- Relationships anticipate the open banquet feast in the Kin-dom. (*Reign of God,* Isa 25:6, Luke 13:29-30)

- Relationships are freed from personal, social, and ecological sin and graced with abundant life for all of creation. (*Good News,* Matt 4:23; 11:4, Mark 1:14-15)

- Relationships are undergirded by just and sustainable resources. (*The Believers Share Their Possessions,* Acts 4:32)

Our freedom to engage in place-making varies. Our roles, status, and abilities in some places may provide great freedom to create and transform places. In other places, our freedom to create and transform place may be limited by prejudices, resources, or dependence on what the status quo provides (e.g., income from a job). When freedom for place-making is limited, place-making may involve creating alternative places—places that resist victimization, develop resiliency, and foster thriving—and, in some cases, moving to new places.

We must be honest that at some point our faithful response to a specific place is to leave that place or put energy in another place in our lives—to shift from roots to routes. Not everyone has the freedom to act on such a choice. They may lack resources, support, or opportunities to leave. They may have obligations, constraints, or fears keeping them in place. Discerning whether to stay in a place requires knowing the difference between self-giving and self-destruction. I do not think God ever calls us to partnership in self-destruction. It may be time to leave a particular place when remaining does harm to ourselves or others. It may be time to leave when God is calling us to a particular place to serve a different group or to take root in a different place where we can flourish. The time to take leave may also arise when the difference made does not justify the cost of remaining. At the same time, we must recognize the work at hand and to which we feel called may involve difficulty, conflict, and struggle—the presence of these does not necessarily mean the absence of calling in a place. Again, a key issue is whether the work is deeply challenging or destructive of self and others.

ATTENDING QUESTIONS

1. How do I see my place(s) in terms of common relational themes in Christianity (e.g., creation, the Great Commission, Great Commandment, Kin-dom of God)?

2. How do I see God already present in my place(s)?

	How do I see God already at work in responding to brokenness and flourishing?
Societally	
Interpersonally	
Intrapersonally	
Ecologically	

3. How might I be in partnership with God's responses to brokenness and flourishing in my place(s)?

	My partnership with God's response to brokenness and flourishing
Societally	
Interpersonally	
Intrapersonally	
Ecologically	

4. Overall, what are my place(s) and what is God calling me to be and do?

5. How is what I bring to place either assets or liabilities to place-making with God?

6. How must I grow in order to respond faithfully to the calls of God and place?

7. Who is with me in my partnership with God?

SUMMARY

A vocation-in-place praxis involves several attending questions. We ask,

- "How is this place claiming me and how do I *belong* (or not)?" to explore dynamics of belonging and alienation, being claimed and rejected, solidarity and indifference, empathy and numbness, agency and powerlessness.

- "What and who is gathered in this place?" to recognize the presence of peoples, creatures, plants, natural environments and habitats, environments built by humans, and sociocultural systems.

- "How is this place gathering me?" to be aware of how place gathers our sense of identity and vocation from our past and from current relationships.

- "What relationships emerge in this place and how do they foster and hinder flourishing of life and Spirit?" to evaluate ways place embodies social brokenness and social flourishing, interpersonal brokenness and interpersonal flourishing, personal brokenness and personal flourishing, and ecological brokenness and ecological flourishing.

- "How am I to be in partnership with God's place-making work?" to partner with God's work in the world through place-making.

Places are not static—they involve movement as well. In the next chapter, we will consider a vocational praxis related to routes that define our places and the ways routes can be places in themselves. Partnership on routes complements place-making with way-making.

FOR REFLECTION

Personal Perspective

1. Describe a place and time when you were working through vocational issues and discernment. What about that place and

what it gathered raised issues? How did you work through those issues—what was your process of discernment?

2. After completing the steps in attending to places we dwell and vocations evoked:

    a. What did you learn overall about your relationships and vocation in place?

    b. In what ways was the process helpful, difficult, or lacking?

    c. Which steps, if any, were particularly meaningful or insightful?

    d. What contribution does place-making make to your vocational imagination?

Leadership Perspective

3. In what ways might you use the steps in attending to place in your roles of leading and educating individuals, groups, and the congregation?

4. What resourcing and equipping might you need to provide support to persons utilizing this process?

5. What do you see as the contributions and limitations of these steps in attending to vocation-in-place?

6. What similarities and differences exist between your usual processes of discernment and that described in this chapter?

7. How might these steps in attending to vocation-in-place connect with existing programs and initiatives you lead (e.g. spiritual gifts, discipleship, outreach, education, volunteer recruitment)?

Congregational Perspective

8. What practices of vocational discernment are common in this congregation? What similarities and differences exist between these and that described in this chapter?

9. How might the approach described in this chapter change the congregation's view of itself, its mission, and way of being in the world?

Chapter 7
ATTENDING TO ROUTES: VOCATION AND CONNECTIONS BETWEEN PLACES

STRANGERS ON ROUTE I-70

There is nothing like being in the same boat to bring people together—or, in this case, a car. I had spent Sunday afternoon in the St. Louis airport waiting for my flight back to Columbus, Ohio. Heavy storms rolled in and out of the area, disrupting flights. Airport restaurants and bars were overflowing. Some tipsy patrons spilled out among several traveling youth sports teams in the waiting area. My flight always showed "on time" until not long before departure. Then it was not. It was cancelled. I queued up with a hundred or more folks to learn our fate. It was late in the evening, and the speculation in line was that we would be stuck for the night. I overheard some people reserving rental cars to give themselves options, and I did the same. As we got closer to the service desk, the word spread that flying out that night was not an option and it might not be until Tuesday morning. Since the cancellation was weather-related, the airline was not going to cover hotels. The man with whom I had been making small talk and I started discussing whether just to drive to Columbus. A woman behind us joined the conversation and we discovered her daughter went to high school with mine. She was in favor of driving as well. We agreed to share a rental car, and then she asked if another woman could join us. A bit before midnight, a sales representative, a pediatrician, a dentistry professor, and a seminary professor hopped into a car heading east.

It was going to be a long night on I-70, so we stopped to grab some snacks and sodas. The pediatrician and the dentist came back with armfuls of junk food. In response to puzzled looks, they shrugged and simply said "job security." The conversation never waned on the drive. Apprehension about keeping the driver awake and the oddity of the situation were a couple of reasons. We each confessed reminding ourselves that everyone had passed TSA security before getting in the car. Curiosity about each other also fueled the conversation. The sales representative was an Ohio State University marching band alum and avid Buckeye fan. The pediatrician was a Michigan State alum and just as avid about the Spartans. The dentistry professor talked about her journey to the faculty of Ohio State from India. Columbus became a topic at one point and the new urban developments transforming run-down neighborhoods. They were puzzled about people being in poverty and homelessness. This sounded like all the problematic attitudes I had heard around gentrification. Could I speak up without angering my travel companions and still get to Columbus?

I diplomatically offered alternative understandings about gentrification and pointed toward underlying assumptions about people and places. Thankfully, the car did not pull off onto the shoulder. My companions respectfully listened and noted my comments as helpful. There was no conversion experience, but they respected me, and I think my comments made a difference. It was still dark when we arrived and did the first drop-off, in one of those gentrified neighborhoods.

This chapter presents a vocational praxis for attending to the routes of life—the forms that place takes in relation to movement and change. The routes we take on a daily basis mark and create the places we dwell. Modes of travel on a route such as a car, bus, train, or plane may function like a mobile place. Sometimes we settle into and dwell on the routes through the twists and turns, joys and sorrows of our life—or as Nelle Morton might say, "the journey is home."[1] We will begin with ways routes create connections and contrasts that make us aware of what place is gathering. Next, we will present a five-step vocation-on-route praxis paralleling that in chapter 6. This praxis explores our connections with routes, raises awareness of the gathering of relationships en route, and claims our partnerships with God en route. Partnership with God in places takes on forms of place-making—in relation to routes that partnership takes the form of way-making.

The route from St. Louis to Columbus that night gathered strangers in a car and their interactions created a place on the move. As we told our stories to each other, the route gathered the past of each individual. The route connected the places of St. Louis and Columbus as well as the neighborhoods of each of us. And when we first arrived in Columbus, we pulled into a place in transition . . . a place on its own route.

MOVING BETWEEN PLACES

In contemporary Western society, we often think of ourselves as always on the move, with hectic lives, mobile lives, transient lives, and displaced lives. So much movement can make people think they have no place they call their own. Place is not the static antithesis of movement. Nomadic peoples move, yet have a sense of place. Israel wandered, was exiled, and experienced diaspora, yet had a profound sense of place. Tim Cresswell suggests that movement actually contributes to the creation of place.[2] As we move from place to place, we develop habits and patterns in that movement. Think about how we form paths in our homes, yards, neighborhoods, offices, campuses, and nature areas. Sometimes we wear a noticeable path in the carpet or the grass (think about the contrast of sidewalks and the paths of students on campuses). Random movement gives way to routes whose patterns take on meaning whether conscious or unconscious, mundane or significant, freely chosen or coerced. Routes gather particular places into habitats, haunts, and territories—and into the places we dwell. In some way, place and routes are the meaning-laden embodiments of space and movement.

Routes, Contrasts, and Connections

To transform space into place, we must engage the relationships and their meaning in a locale. Such engagement requires some degree of time and presence. This is easy to imagine as we consider dwelling in a particular place. It is harder to picture in the midst of movement, yet it is possible. Morton points out there is a way that the journeying can become home. The idea of *flow* involves a heightened awareness and time seemingly slowing in the midst of intense activity.[3] We can also think of forms of spirituality where mindfulness in motion unites thought and action into one.

Time and presence are essential and *necessary* aspects of place-making, but they may not be *sufficient* aspects because familiarity can create obliviousness and spiritual slumber. Place-related practices such as those in the prior chapter may work against obliviousness, but we need more. Our awareness of things arises from contrasts and connections. Attending to routes between places contributes these necessary things to our awareness of place and our ability to learn and grow.

In the absence of contrasts, we would not be able to distinguish one thing from another. Think about times you could not recognize the difference in how things look, taste, feel, smell, or sound. Sometimes that is a matter of inattentiveness, sometimes it is about our projecting sameness onto situations, and at other times distinctions are subtle enough to demand training in a craft or discipline to perceive them. Think about times when you became self-aware about some aspects of yourself. Most likely, that awareness came in encounters with people who were not like you in some way. Being a minority in a context creates heightened awareness of oneself and the majority group. Max Müller's adage that knowing just one religion means knowing none is apt in many aspects of life. We do not know our own culture, religion, gender, language, or place without knowing other ones. We can know ourselves as we experience the contrasts in our identity that arise in differing places. We can know our place and others places because our routes associate places in ways we can experience their contrasts.

In the absence of connections, we would not develop meanings between that which is in contrast. The connecting work of routes is the gathering work of place: a relational way of being. Just because we can distinguish between what we see, taste, feel, smell, or hear does not mean we recognize connections between them that lead to their meaningfulness. The connections perceived between sounds lead to whether we experience them as language, music, nonsense, or noise. The significance of a particular event is deeply connected with its broader historical context. The meaning of a biblical text is connected with the preceding and following texts. Imagination and meaning-making are all about recognizing connections between things. We can discover the significance of our place and others' places because our routes connect these places in ways where we can discover meanings. The *ways* that routes connect places contribute to meaning making too. The connections made between the same places by movement via foot, bike, bus, train, car, plane, ship, or internet are different.

As we think about routes, we should keep in mind routes through time as well as routes through physical space. We need to consider the contrasts and connections of routes between places in our psychological, developmental, spiritual, and social life journeys.

Our dwelling is a network of places bound together by our routes. If routes involve difference and connections, then we need to ask *between what places* we move, *how* we move between places, and *why* we take particular routes (as opposed to other routes).

Attending to Connections between Places and Vocations Evoked

If routes contribute to forming place and place evokes vocation, then attending to our routes also becomes integral to vocational discernment. Such discernment involves the following:

- Attending to connections on routes by asking, "How do routes between particular places claim me and how do I belong (or not)?"

- Attending to the gathering of routes by asking, "What and who is contrasted and connected by my routes between particular places?"

- Attending to our identity and vocational narratives by asking, "How are these routes between particular places differentiating and connecting me?"

- Attending to grace and brokenness by asking, "How do routes between particular places foster and hinder flourishing of life and Spirit?"

- Attending to our role in forming relationships by asking, "How am I to be in partnership with God's way-making work?"

HOW DO ROUTES BETWEEN PARTICULAR PLACES CLAIM ME AND HOW DO I BELONG (OR NOT)?

Western individualism celebrates the heroic self who leaves home on a quest (or conquest) bravely facing and overcoming challenges alone. Yet, typically stories of such ventures have the hero or heroine assisted by someone or something just when needed. We rarely, if ever, totally move and travel alone (especially now with GPS). We exist in a web of relationships on our routes, so we need to consider the ways we are connected to the spaces we travel through and to others traveling with us as we move. We might think of any number of biblical journeys reflecting relationships en route—Noah and the ark; Israel in exodus, wilderness, and exile; the Good Samaritan; Jesus in the wilderness (something was tempting him...he was not in a vacuum); the road to Emmaus; the travels of Paul. In times of trial, knowing we are not going through something alone is a key to resilience—others have trod the stony road. How we experience our connections shapes our motivations, actions, satisfaction, resilience, and resolve relative to both routes and God-in-place.

We need to consider connectedness in terms of belonging, solidarity, empathy, being claimed, and agency. Tensions exist in each of these categories because our sense of connectedness differs from route to route and varies over time. We live in the tensions of belonging and alienation, bridging and isolation, solidarity and indifference, empathy and numbness, agency and powerlessness.

Belonging ←→Alienation

Whether our movement is by choice or coercion, being en route involves displacement and with that a level of vulnerability. The vulnerability in being a traveler is part of why hospitality is such an important practice in many cultures. The more we feel safe (even if challenged) on a route, the more likely we are to have a sense of belonging—being on the right path even if we are unsure where the path is leading. The more we feel threatened on a route, the more likely we are to sense alienation from what we encounter on the path and wish for the end of the trek. For some, the threat and alienation of a route never seem to end.

Another clue to belonging and alienation on a route may be found in how we experience departing a place. As we depart, what is the mix of feeling loss for what is left behind and feeling anticipation for the travel ahead? Do we feel most "ourselves" dwelling or journeying?

Bridging ←→ Isolation

Routes can claim us when we have an openness to sharing in how they bridge and connect different places. While our travel may be wrapped up in personal pursuits, the routes we take are not ours alone—they are part of what forms a network of places. I doubt that we are often conscious of our role in this bridging dynamic and perhaps we may actively work against it. We may wish to isolate some places from others for the sake of safety, balance, simplicity, integrity, or Sabbath.

Solidarity ←→ Indifference

Recognition of a common cause with others influences the degree to which we have solidarity with or indifference toward others. In terms of travel, this may become a matter of seeing things as a cooperative journey or a competitive race. Consider how people respond to auto or foot traffic congestion. Sometimes people respond with cooperation, letting others merge or cut across one's path with patience—reflecting, in a way, the popular saying from Ram Dass: "we're just walking each other home." At other times, people respond with competitive indifference, racing to cut off others or expressing fits of rage.

Empathy ←→ Apathy

Identification with the experiences of others influences the extent we have empathy with or numbness toward others. In terms of travel, I suspect this may be a matter of how open we are to interruptions, detours, stoppages, and side trips. When travel is merely streamlined transport between places, we become insular and resist interruptions that allow us to identify with others. When travel is a journey or a way-making,[4] we become present to others on and along our routes.

Agency ←→ Powerlessness

A very important factor in our connections with a route is our freedom. This involves the freedom to choose whether to be en route. Do we have agency and means to travel or does a lack of power expose us to coerced travel? This also involves the freedom to shape the nature of the route. Do we have agency and means to choose how and where we travel, or does a lack of power subject us to predetermined routes?

Our sense of connectedness plays a significant role in our sense of vocation and routes. When the majority of categories for understanding our connectedness with routes are positive, we are likely to delve more deeply into our partnership with God en route. When the opposite is true we tend to question, with good reason, whether we left God behind somewhere along the way. Just because a route is a stony road, we should not confuse the presence of difficulty, conflict, and struggle with the absence of calling en route—sometimes those are part of the work at hand.

ATTENDING QUESTIONS

1. What are my experiences of this route relative to the categories of belonging, being claimed, solidarity, empathy and agency?

	Degree that I experience	How I experience	Source of experience
Belonging and alienation			
Bridging and isolation			
Solidarity with and indifference to others			
Empathy and emotional numbness toward others			
Agency and powerlessness			

2. To what extent is the combined experience across these categories positive? How does this provide joy and draw you more deeply into the journey and partnership with God there?

3. To what extent is the combined experience across these categories negative? How does this shape your view of vocation and routes as the following:

   a. Satisfying

   b. A duty

   c. Struggle for a greater purpose and/or personal growth

   d. Self-giving

   e. Self-destructive and not worth the cost

   f. Misplaced and leading to a search for an alternative route

4. How do the webs of emotional dynamics relative to both routes and God-in-place influence your motivations, actions, satisfaction, resilience, and resolve for vocation on this route?

5. Who am I passing by or stopping for on this route?

WHAT AND WHO IS CONTRASTED AND CONNECTED BY MY ROUTES BETWEEN PARTICULAR PLACES?

If answering the question of what is gathered is difficult for the places we *dwell*, it may seem even more so in terms of what our *routes* connect and gather. Perhaps we become caught up in our haste to arrive. Perhaps the routine of our transportation allows us to daydream, worry, converse, or bebop along in a different world. Perhaps too much passes by too quickly to take in. We may be so not present that we arrive at a place unsettled by the awareness that we have no clue how we got there, hoping we did no harm on the way. Attending to what is connected and gathered by our routes involves a kind of bi-focal vision. We need to see the overall patterns of our routes and we need to see up close what is on our routes.

We attend to the connections of our routes with varying breadth of scope. The broadest scope to consider is the general network of our routes—how they weave together as a whole. The narrowest scope might be the paths we take from room to room. Between these extremes are all the particular routes between and within the places we dwell—home, office, classroom, congregation, neighborhoods, communities, and regions.

We attend to what we encounter on our routes through several categories. Utilizing multiple categories helps us pay attention comprehensively. We look for the peoples, creatures, plants, natural environments, built environments, sociocultural dimensions, and embodiments manifest on routes.

We attend to routes by considering the aspects of the routes we travel. We consider origins and destinations, the mode of travel, frequency of taking a route, when we travel, the purposes of travel, and who/what travels with us. Some modes of travel, such as with our car or a spot on the bus/subway/train, actually become moving places and should be explored as such.

ATTENDING QUESTIONS

1. What places does this particular route connect?

2. What mode of travel do I use on this route?

3. With whom and what am I traveling on this route? Consider things present through radio, phone, and media devices. Consider what you carry with you and what is in the transport with you.

4. What am I passing by on this route? Consider peoples, creatures, plants, natural and built environments, sociocultural structures.

5. What stops and side trips are typically part of this route?

6. What do I encounter through the senses (sight, smell, taste, touch, sound) on this route?

HOW ARE THESE ROUTES BETWEEN PARTICULAR PLACES DIFFERENTIATING AND CONNECTING ME?

As we considered the similar question in relation to dwelling, I suggested that we form our self and our vocation from the relationships and past experiences gathered by place. What about the routes between such places? Are identity and vocation independent of routes? Perhaps so, if on our routes we slip into or seek out anonymity. However, routes between places may contribute to our identity in at least three ways.

Routes as a "Place" of Identity Formation

If it is true that existence always happens in a place, then our being on a route has some qualities of a place. We are always some place, but not all places significantly influence our identity. Some routes define our

135

identity through their intensity and duration while others by their repetition and familiarity; the journey becomes a dwelling of sorts. The Middle Passage, the Underground Railroad, the Trail of Tears, forty-years in the wilderness, and the journey of a refugee are examples of intense routes taking on characteristics of place. The drive to a favorite getaway, the daily commute, routine work trips, and the family getting almost anywhere together (and surviving) are examples of familiar routes that have a sense of formative "place" to us.

Routes Raising Awareness of Identities

The contrasts and connections between places that routes create may make us more conscious of our identity (or identities). This is particularly true when routes take us to places where we have different roles and responsibilities, use different abilities, have different experiences of enjoyment and freedom, or shift between majority and minority status.

Routes through Time (Trajectory of Identity and Vocation)

Routes are not just physical movements. We can also think of our routes through time and history within a place. In this sense, the contrasts and connections between experiences in a particular place may make us aware of the trajectory of our identity and vocation over time.

ATTENDING QUESTIONS

1. To what degree do I feel or try to be anonymous on this route?

2. How does the intensity or duration of this route form my sense of self?

3. When and how often do I take this route?

4. How does the familiarity of this route form my sense of self?

5. How do particular routes connect with each other to form a network of places?

6. How do particular routes come together to define the place I dwell?

7. How does this route help transition me between my identities in various places?

8. What parts of me do I leave behind when I take a route away from a place?

9. Who am I while on this route?

One way to raise consciousness about how routes shape us is to experiment with using different routes and modes of transportation. If you typically take the interstate, try a surface road. If you drive, try taking a bus or subway, or try walking or biking. If you fly, drive or take a train. After changing routes or mode of transportation, compare the experiences and your sense of self on that journey.

HOW DO ROUTES BETWEEN PARTICULAR PLACES FOSTER AND HINDER FLOURISHING OF LIFE AND THE SPIRIT?

We now need to transition from various descriptions of routes to evaluating how well life and the Spirit flourish on our routes. Such evaluation requires humility and courage, appreciation and critique, awareness of complexity, and intentional methodology. In the previous chapter, we considered brokenness and flourishing of life and the Spirit in social, interpersonal, personal, and ecological ways. The dynamics leading to brokenness and flourishing in place exist in routes as well, although in different forms.

Social Brokenness ←→ Social Flourishing

How do sociocultural systems help and hinder flourishing of life and the Spirit on routes? They hinder flourishing of life and the Spirit when such systems as racism, sexism, classism, anthropocentrism, heterosexism, and ableism, along with their intersections, break relationships and dehumanize. We can make others an object of entertainment when we travel to take in their culture or take pity on their situation.[5] We can make others into predators lying in wait on our routes.[6] We can make exiles and refugees into marauders, even though social brokenness forces or makes their travel necessary. We can whitewash enslavement and trafficking as some form of immigration. We can make others into enemies in the friction between globalization and the localism.

Social and cultural systems help flourishing of life and the Spirit when they resist objectification and foster human and ecological relationships. This involves the ability to embody welcome and offer hospitality to the stranger and co-traveler, the capacity to remember when we were vulnerable en route, and vision to see commonality in the midst of our different pursuits.

We need only remember God's concern for the alien and those put out to recognize the spiritual grounding of social relationships. The prophets condemned Israel for idolatry, but they equally challenged Israel's forgetfulness of its dependence on God en route.

Interpersonal Brokenness ←→ *Interpersonal Flourishing*

On our routes, we engage specific persons and aspects of creation. As noted in the last chapter, our personal relationships will, to varying degrees, both reflect and challenge prevailing sociocultural and ecological systems. How do interpersonal dynamics help and hinder flourishing of life and the Spirit? They hinder flourishing of life and the Spirit as they break interpersonal relationships through acts of emotional and physical harm. We may tend to do things as a traveler we would not do where we dwell. An increased tendency to do harm en route may arise for various reasons. We may feel free from the accountability created by not seeing another again or by the anonymity of travel. However, one never knows when you might pass this way again or when you are going to need help. Travel can be frustrating and draining, lowering tolerance and the thresholds for acting out in anger, even rage. When we feel vulnerable en route, we may imagine motivations behind actions are hostile and thus warrant harming responses. The lack of resources on the route may make us act out of need and desperation.

Interpersonal dynamics help flourishing of life and the Spirit when we see our routes as gathering relationships, a key aspect of place, rather than relational dead space between places. Travel is another way of being in the world relationally. When we are in the places we dwell, those we do not know are the strangers, and flourishing depends on our hospitality and welcome. When we are en route, the tables are turned. *We* are the stranger, the strange one, and flourishing depends on our being good guests.

We need only remember how often in the biblical witness that prophetic messages, revelation, divine visitation, incarnation, and good news come in the form of a stranger. In particular, the Emmaus road story is paradigmatic of routes blessed with such things.

Personal Brokenness ←→ Personal Flourishing

Intrapersonally, we engage the inner relationships of our personal history en route. How do intrapersonal dynamics help and hinder flourishing of life and the Spirit? We may struggle to flourish on our routes for several reasons. We struggle when our routes fragment our sense of self rather than weave our identities in place together. We do not flourish when we lose ourselves in the anonymity and fog of travel. We languish when travel triggers past trauma and fears close us off from gifts of the path. We falter when routes become flight from difficult personal matters in our lives.

We flourish in life and in the Spirit as we open ourselves to the blessings and potential for growth and redemption on the route—when we say yes to God's call forward. For good reason, the metaphor of journey may be the predominant metaphor for thinking about personal and faith development. However, embracing our routes does not negate the importance of dwelling in our places. Personal development, learning, and growth depend on the stimulation, adventure, and novelty of various routes. Moving into redemptive new ways of being requires a productive level of dissonance that disrupts our habituation to past ways. The staying power of these new ways necessitates integrating the rhythms of our dwellings and our routes.

We need only remember that God's unconditional love never flees or falters to recognize the grounding of our spiritual lives en route. We are in God where we dwell and where we move. Following God into our routes and flourishing there takes courage and openness to the challenges and adventures of routes. Routes make us prone to fears, but courage, faith and God's unconditional love frees us to *have* fears without *being* them.[7] God's perfect love casts out the debilitating fear that freezes us in place and the past.

Ecological Brokenness ◄► Ecological Flourishing

Thinking in terms of routes pushes us to evaluate our relationships with the rest of creation as part of our partnership with God in place. How do ecological dynamics help and hinder flourishing of *all* life and the Spirit? Human activity en route threatens ecological well-being when the environment is merely the scenery along human routes. The idea that our path on earth is a temporary one leading to a grander and eternal spiritual home in heaven reflects this attitude. In this scenario, humans may decide they need not care about the environment because it is a disposable resource to be left behind. Human activity also threatens ecological flourishing when humans view the environment as an obstacle to our destination and goals. Humans are prone to create routes that destroy the environment.

Creation flourishes when our gratitude and respect for the environment makes our movements that of guests rather than conquerors. Our movements should flow *with* rather than against ecological environments. This is not to say we should not shape our environments, but rather we should do so in *harmony* with the environment. Our ecological footprint should be small where we dwell, but it should also be light as we move.[8]

To recognize the spiritual grounding of routes amid ecological environs we need only remember that after placing humanity in garden of creation God experienced and enjoyed the garden by roaming in it (Gen 3:8). Like us, God continues to tend to creation as God journeys in and through it.

ATTENDING QUESTIONS

1. In what ways do I recognize or experience brokenness on my routes?

	Signs of brokenness	Causes for brokenness
Social		
Interpersonal		
Intrapersonal		
Ecological		

2. In what ways do I recognize or experience flourishing on my routes?

	Signs of flourishing	Sources of flourishing
Social		
Interpersonal		
Intrapersonal		
Ecological		

3. What graces and assets for flourishing of life and the Spirit are present on my routes?

	Signs of grace	Assets/resources for flourishing
Social		
Interpersonal		
Intrapersonal		
Ecological		

WAY-MAKING: HOW AM I TO BE IN PARTNERSHIP WITH GOD ON THIS ROUTE?

God is relational and God's work in the world is very much about forging right relationships. Those relationships are between God and the whole of creation, between humans, and between humans and the rest of creation. The touchstones of the Great Commandment, the Great Commission, the Kin-dom of God, and many aspects of Christianity point to this. Our vocations then are rooted in the nature of relationships, whether those are gathered by a particular place or by a particular route. Place is the gathering of those concrete mutual relationships that influence us and that we can influence—the relationships in which being a neighbor is possible to realize. Routes are movements between places, evolutions of a place over time, and gatherings of the places we dwell.

The gathering God who is *I Am—Place* is also the connecting and transforming God who is a way-maker—a God on the move with creation. As way-maker, God creates possibilities for growth, flourishing, and agency. As way-maker, God sees beyond brokenness and crosses the borders of all that divides, enslaves, and thwarts life—God redeems by finding ways out of no-ways. As way-maker, God sustains the alien, exile, sojourner, explorer, and pilgrim on the paved path and the stony road. In addition to God's ability to gather everything for the glory of God and the good of all creation, God's freedom for the future is God's sovereignty and holiness. While in relationship with the world and thus *conditioned* by it, God *is not determined* by the world and the way things are. In every moment of experience, God is offering a way to move into the future creatively and redemptively. God's freedom allows unfettered pursuit of God's purposes. As our growth with and in God unfolds, we also have greater freedom to be in partnership with God's work. That increasing freedom, being unencumbered by the past for God's purposes, is the process of sanctification. If we are to be in partnership with God in making ways for right relationships that lead to flourishing, we must also take part in God's work of connecting and transforming.

As we continually transform the relationships in places and routes, we engage in *way-making*. The key vocational,[9] spiritual, and ethical questions are whether our way-making is a faithful response to the call of God en route. Does our way-making reflect God's desire for the nature of relationships between God and people, God and creation, self and neighbor, and humans and creation? Is our transforming of personal, social, spiritual, and ecological relationships en route consistent with what we believe God is doing in the world? I suggest the following as some themes shaping Christian imaginations about faithful way-making toward the Kin-dom of God:

- Routes to the Kin-dom include ways God undermines power by using the least expected persons to do God's work.

- Routes to the Kind-dom redeem the past in ways that create freedom for the future and the works of God.

- Routes to the Kin-dom turn strangers into co-travelers.

- Routes to the Kin-dom pass through both green pastures and the shadow of death.

- Routes to the Kin-dom involve trust and faith based in an accrued confidence that nothing can separate us from the unconditional love of God.

- Routes to the Kin-dom forge justice and peace.

- Routes to the Kin-dom cross borders of destructive and sinful division.

- Routes to the Kin-dom connect places to allow mutual love, respect, and empathy between others and creation.

- Routes to the Kin-dom reflect the life and way of Jesus.

- Routes to the Kin-dom gather those in diaspora, in exile, out of place, and in wilderness.

- Routes to the Kin-dom lead to dwelling with God.

At some point, our faithful response to our routes and God may be to stop and take root in place—to shift from routes to roots, even if only for a while, if persons have such freedom. Dwelling provides rest from the journey. It is also an antidote to routes being means of avoidance rather than wholeness. However deep roots may be, they provide references and resources for our routes and opportunities for being deepening relationships.

ATTENDING QUESTIONS

1. How do I see my routes in relation to faithful way-making toward the Kin-dom of God?

2. How do I see God already present in my routes?

	How do I see God already at work responding to brokenness and flourishing?
Societally	
Interpersonally	
Intrapersonally	
Ecologically	

3. How might I be in partnership with God's responses to brokenness and flourishing in my routes?

	My partnership with God's response to brokenness and flourishing
Societally	
Interpersonally	
Intrapersonally	
Ecologically	

4. Overall, what are my routes and what is God calling me to be and do?

5. How are what I bring to routes either assets or liabilities to way-making with God?

6. How must I grow in order to respond faithfully to the calls of God and routes?

7. Who is with me in my partnership with God?

SUMMARY

A vocation-en-route praxis incorporates several attending questions. We ask the following:

- "How do routes between particular places claim me and how do I *belong* (or not)?" to explore belonging and alienation, bridging and isolation, solidarity and indifference, empathy and apathy, and agency and powerlessness.

- "What and who is contrasted and connected by my routes between particular places?" to recognize ways places are woven together and what we are passing on our routes.

- "How are these routes between particular places differentiating and connecting me?" to understand the ways routes form identity, make us aware of various aspects of our identities, and link past and present vocation.

- "How do routes between particular places foster and hinder flourishing of life and Spirit?" to evaluate ways routes hold social brokenness and social flourishing, interpersonal brokenness and interpersonal flourishing, personal brokenness and personal flourishing, and ecological brokenness and ecological flourishing.

- "How am I to be in partnership with God?" to partner with God's work in the world through way-making.

With vocation-in-place and vocation-en-route praxes in mind, we now need to consider implications for forming vocational imagination. In the concluding chapter, we will do so in relation to practical theology and forming vocational imagination in faith communities.

FOR REFLECTION

Personal Perspective

1. Describe a route or transition when you were working through vocational issues and discernment. What about that route or transition raised issues? How did you work through those issues—what was your process of discernment?

2. How is attending to routes in life different from attending to the places we dwell?

3. After completing the steps in attending to routes of life and vocations evoked:

   a. What did you learn overall about your relationships and vocation en route?

   b. In what ways was the process helpful, difficult, or lacking?

   c. Which steps, if any, were particularly meaningful or insightful?

4. What does the idea of way-making contribute to your vocational imagination?

Leadership Perspective

5. In what ways might you use the steps in attending to routes and transition in your roles of leading and educating individuals, groups, and the congregation?

6. What resourcing and equipping might you need to provide support to persons utilizing this process?

7. What do you see as the contributions and limitations of these steps in attending to vocation-en-route?

8. What similarities and differences exist between your usual processes of discernment and that described in this chapter?

9. How might these steps in attending to vocation-en-route connect with existing programs and initiatives you lead (e.g. spiritual gifts, discipleship, outreach, education, volunteer recruitment)?

Congregational Perspective

10. What practices of vocational discernment are common in this congregation? What similarities and differences exist between these and that described in this chapter?

11. How might the approach described in this chapter change the congregation's view of itself, its mission, and way of being in the world?

Chapter 8
GATHERING SAINTS: FOSTERING VOCATIONAL IMAGINATION

I have sought to address aspects of failed vocational imagination by exploring the relational work of God in the world, assumptions about the nature of vocation, and the ways vocation emerges in places and routes. Closely attending to the places we dwell and the routes we take helps us discern the calling of God into the work of place-making and way-making So, how might this come together in ways that help us foster vocational imagination in place? One way is to recognize vocation-in-place as the practical theology of daily life. A second way is to consider the implications for leaders and educators in faith communities.

PRACTICAL THEOLOGY AS VOCATIONAL THEOLOGY

Practical theology, in very general terms, addresses the interplay of theology and context. It is both an academic discipline and *something practiced consciously and unconsciously by Christians in daily life*. Practical theology is often confused with applied theology, but their relationship with context makes them distinct from each other. *Applied theology* seeks to take a set of beliefs, scripture, practices, and attitudes and make them operational in and applicable to a context—the relationship between theology and context is unilateral. In *practical theology* models, the relationship is bi-directional. An example of this kind of relationship is Don Browning's revised correlational model in which theology and context are put into mutual dialogue. The model is correlational in that theology raises issues about context, and context raises issues about theology.[1] Another example is the praxis model in which the interplay of theology and context is a matter of reflective action. Beliefs from the context and its larger tradition shape action in context, and the actions in context shape beliefs in a cyclical manner. Thomas Groome's influential shared praxis model reflects this approach.[2]

Interpretation is central to the tasks of practical theology and to vocation-in-place, although in the latter people may instead speak in terms of discernment. In general, our practices of interpretation require an openness to the address of what we are interpreting, awareness of what is shaping our interpretation, intentional methodology combined with artfulness and creativity, capacity to evaluate and choose between multiple interpretations, sensitivity to the Spirit, and a diverse community sharing in the interpretive practice. Interpretation is a living, open-ended process, a keen attentiveness birthed by disciplines of study and spirituality. Becoming a good interpreter is a key task in practical theology. Because interpretation shapes understanding that leads to actions and attitudes (and vice versa), interpretation is an ethical enterprise. Reading a text or context is an ethical act.[3]

Exploring the dynamics between vocation and place generates three results. One is a preliminary practical theology *of* place where place *and vocation* are subjects of reflection. A second result is taking place as the arena for practical theology where place reframes the central categories of context and situation in practical theology. A third result is to consider practical theology as vocational theology.

Practical Theology of Place and Vocation

It is difficult these days for me to separate place and vocation—they are deeply intertwined. The descriptions of place, vocation, God's gathering work, the self, and engagement of place come together into practical theology of place and vocation. Several general assumptions are very important for the way I suggest attending to roots and routes, and the callings they evoke:

- An essential aspect of the places we dwell and the routes we travel is their power to gather.

- What is gathered is deeply interconnected, whether helpfully or harmfully.

- What is gathered is in a continual process of individually and collectively becoming—a continual process of creation by God.

- Continuity within the processes of becoming can mislead us into thinking places, identities, and vocation are static things.

- Partnership is a defining feature of the way that God calls us into relationship and into the future.

- Imagination shapes our capacity for recognizing connectedness and meaning-making.

- Empathy, or the lack thereof, significantly shapes motivations for relationships and vocation.

Place is a continual process of gathering particular groups of people, creatures, plants, climate, and physical structures. It is the evolving web of relationships between God, humans, and creation—the relationships from which we come to be and to which we contribute. Shaped by culture and practices, "place" is the way we imagine this localized web and our position in it—our relational way of being in the world.

Vocation is partnership with God's work in and for the world within particular places and routes. The call to partnership comes from God; however, the places we dwell and the routes we travel evoke it. This means vocation is always changing and evolving. However, over time and across the places of daily life and our lives, we come to recognize a pattern and trajectory in how we partner with God in the world. Rooted in the concrete elements of a place, vocation responds to God's vision for forming relationships reflective of God's Kin-dom.

The self is a process—the continuity of individual moments of experience over time. In each moment of experience, the self emerges from and in response to what place gathers, and God offers the most whole and redemptive way to emerge. This dynamic ties together the relationships in places and on routes with the ongoing and immediate calling of God. Stories we tell about ourselves, drawn from the places we dwell, create the continuity of self and vocation we experience over time.

If we are in partnership with God, we must ask what the God with whom we partner is doing in the world. The diversity of traditions within Christianity means there is no simple answer to this question. Major themes in the tradition include the Great Commission, the Great Commandment, the Kin-dom of God, and the creating, redeeming, and sustaining nature of God. Generalization risks reductionism, but two threads connecting these themes are desires for right relationships and for flourishing of life and the Spirit—flourishing of both humans and all of creation. To pursue these desires, we need to address the social, interpersonal, personal, and ecological grace and brokenness present. As place-maker and way-maker, God creatively gathers graces and brokenness in ways leading to fullness of physical and spiritual life.

Attentiveness to how we dwell in places helps us recognize the callings evoked by *I Am—Place*. *Moving* along routes provides us with contrasts and connections to be conscious of callings evoked by *I Am—Way-maker*. Engaging places and routes involves a theological and vocational praxis of the following:

- Naming the connections one has with place and routes with particular attention to affective and emotional dimensions

- Identifying what and who is gathered in place and on routes

- Recognizing the ways that a place and a route gather our past and current aspects of our identity

- Critically reflecting on the relationships of a place and a route in terms of how they reflect grace and brokenness, and embody flourishing of life and the Spirit

- Partnering in God's gathering work of place-making and way-making

Including a step in this process addressing affective connections to place and routes (e.g., empathy and alienation) is an important addition to practical theology models. While solidarity with a context or issue may be implied in praxis models, it is rarely addressed explicitly. Including affect brings attention to factors of motivation and commitment in praxis and mitigates praxis becoming a merely a problem-solving exercise.

A practical theology of place and vocation uses *gathering* as a central lens for critical reflection. God's ability to gather for the purposes of God and the flourishing of all creation is a central feature of God's holiness. In every moment of experience, God creatively offers a way for persons and communities—creatures and ecologies—to gather their pasts in ways that are creative, redemptive, sustaining, and liberative. Such gathering holiness confronts the gathering of barriers, control, conquest, and empire. Such gathering holiness transforms personal, social, and ecological ways of being—rather than include others into the status quo, we create anew ways to be in relationship. Such gathering holiness is the unfolding route toward the place of the Kin-dom of God.

Too often, we limit our imagination of grace to freedom from condemnation, freedom from getting the consequences we deserve. However, grace is also the blessing of what we need to survive, thrive, and serve. In a sense, gathering is a grace-full work that is creative, redemptive, and liberative. We experience prevenient grace in the encounter of *I Am—Place*, the ground of gathering places, who gathers the world into being. We experience redemptive grace as God gathers brokenness and blessing into personal, social, and ecological wholeness. We experience sanctifying grace in the encounter with *I Am—Way-maker*, the way of liberating routes, who increases our freedom for partnering with God's work in the world.

Holiness and grace rooted in gathering stand in contrast to that based in purging to be pure. There are a variety of things that Christians understand as counter to God's will and impeding our relationships with God, neighbor, and creation. However, there is a difference between letting go of such encumbrances and purging them. In some ways, purging does not provide us freedom because there is always something that must be controlled and put out. There is a difference between shedding things impeding our partnership with God and purging our fears about ourselves and our relationship with God. The former is seeking freedom *for* God and the latter is seeking freedom *from* anxiety about ourselves.

Place as Arena of Practical Theology

Place may be treated as the object of practical theology engagement as in a practical theology *of* place. However, place is also a conceptual framework capable of shaping practical theology. It may do so by redefining the categories of context and situation that are central in practical theology.

While sharing many of their features, place is not just another way of talking about contexts and situations. Place is more akin to a way-of-being-in-the-world than sets of analytical categories and factors conditioning action associated with context and situation. When we talk about *context*, we address questions of how a particular set of dynamics, issues, beliefs, and practices come together to shape interpretations and actions. In the case of interpreting a text, we need to know its historical, cultural, literary, religious, and canonical contexts. In the case of a ministry setting, we know what "works" in one congregation does not necessarily mean it is effective or appropriate in another. We need to consider congregational culture, history, civic relationships, and power structures. Theological and professional education are very concerned with connecting academic contexts with the contexts in which reflection and practice take place. Context conditions our thinking and doing, but we tend to address it as the stage of our activities, something to which we adapt.

When we talk of *situations*, we address a combination of dynamics that compel some reaction. Edward Farley describes situations as

> the way various items, powers, and events in the environment gather together so as to require responses from participants. In this sense, any living, perhaps any actual, entity exists in situations. Situations like reality itself are never static. Living beings, we might say, live in their environments (contexts) in continuing responses to ever-changing, ever-forming situations. Situations can be very brief in time (such as a thunderstorm or a marital quarrel) or very protracted (such as the Western epoch, the nuclear age).[4]

Professional education seeks to equip persons with insights, skills, and attitudes that enable them to address situations. Case studies are classic mechanisms for developing such abilities. However, we tend to address situations as particular dilemmas and problems—consider, for example, the phrase, "we have a situation here."

Mary McClintock Fulkerson writes that place both frames[5] and describes situations.[6] Understanding place "as a structure of lived, corporate, and bodied experience,"[7] she argues, "the categories of place, in short, are best designed to display the shape of faith as a lived *situation*"[8] by bringing into view the "complexities of bodied, visceral, local, and global environment" in situations.[9] For McClintock Fulkerson, place advances contextual and situational thinking by

- Attending to embodied experience shaped by culture

- Transcending "the dualisms of mind-body, mental-physical, and self-world"[10]

- Taking "seriously the full continuum of human experience, particularly the non-discursive ordering that constitutes place,"[11] and this includes the affective dimension

- Dealing with more than the immediacies of situations

In addition to these contributions, I think place raises our awareness of the interplay between humans, creatures, ecological environments, and built environments in ways that context and situations do not.

Place evokes us into partnerships to form a web of relationships that is more than being evoked to resolve a situation.[12]

Vocational Theology

We can think of place as an *object of* practical theology and as a *framework for* practical theology. Can we imagine the dynamics of place transforming practical theology into vocational theology?

I think that a common concern in practical theology is faithful change. We may seek to change a situation in light of faithfulness to a tradition and its vision for the future. The interplay of situation and tradition may initiate change in some aspect of belief, practice, or attitudes of individuals. Situations may cause the reconsideration of traditions and lead to change in them.

Practical theology is a process of discerning individual and corporate partnership with God's activity in the world (i.e., vocation) at the intersections of tradition (scripture and history), the contemporary world, and the urging of the Spirit toward the Kin-dom of God. Closely connected with discernment of vocation are the formation of Christian identity, imagination, and faith manifest in thought, attitude, and action. Practical theology is practiced by persons in all stations and stages of life. Recognizing that laity, professionals, and clergy all engage in practical theology, leaders and teachers are responsible for equipping those in their care with resources, practices, and skills for lifelong vocation in its varied embodiments.

The praxis I propose for engaging place reflects a practical theology that is at the same time vocational theology. This praxis begins with naming our connections with place, then proceeding to name the ways place gathers others and ourselves, assessing the grace and brokenness of relationships in that gathering, and finally responding to the call of God-in-place to embody glimpses of the Kin-dom of God. Description and analysis in practical theology are connected in some way to theologically informed action in context. If we understand such action to be responsiveness to God in context, then I think we may understand practical theology as vocational theology.

This means that to foster vocation, the equipping ministries of congregations (combination of leadership, education, and formation) need to include developing the capacities of persons to engage in everyday forms of practical-vocational theology.

IMPLICATIONS FOR CONGREGATIONAL LEADERSHIP

The responsibilities of ordained, professional, and lay leaders of faith communities include equipping persons for their individual vocations. Leadership always includes educational components, whether in the pulpit, meeting room, fellowship hall, classroom, nursery, narthex, or office. An effective missional organization is also an effective learning organization. To explore the implications of place on equipping faith communities for vocation, we need to consider calling into a place of leadership, how we think of congregations as places in themselves, goals of equipping ministry, and approaches to fostering vocation-in-place.

Called to a Place

I have addressed vocation mainly in terms of the places and the routes of daily life where we find ourselves. In doing so, I note there are times when we leave a place because we cannot flourish there or because we need opportunities for growth. There are also times when a new place calls us and not just as an exit from where we currently are. Congregations are among those places calling and gathering persons to it as members and as leaders. For those in ordained and professional ministries, this involves denominational appointment to a congregation or congregational calling to a position of leadership within it. For other leaders it may be a matter of moving into a staff position or committee chair from within the congregation.

Over time, a pattern tends to emerge in the ways we partner with God in our places and on our routes of life. We may tend to partner in forms of leadership, healing, advocacy, equipping, reconciliation, and prayer, among others. These habits are the continuity of partnership with God we most often have in mind when using the term *vocation*. Mentors, teachers, pastors, counselors, family, friends, community members, and ordination committees help us discern these patterns in partnership. Again, we must remember that continuity does not make vocation a thing to have—vocation remains a process. Our habits of partnership with God accumulate assets enabling deeper and more effective vocation. Such assets include abilities, expertise, experiences, wisdom, spirituality, passion, and confidence. As we and those around us recognize habits in our partnership with God, we may choose to be more intentional in nurturing the knowledge, skills, attitudes, and spirituality that deepen our capacity for vocation across places and routes.

God's gathering work in place-making and way-making is not limited to what a place or route currently holds. God also gathers resources and assets for flourishing of life and the Spirit to places and routes—God calls or gathers people to new places and routes. This may happen through physically moving from one place to another or through moving to a new "place" of responsibility within a place. Those responsible for appointments, searches, and nominations are important participants in discerning ways God is gathering gifts and graces for God's work in a place.

CONGREGATIONS, PLACES, AND ROUTES

As we seek to foster vocation-in-place, we need to consider ways that congregations in themselves are places and parts of routes.

Congregations as a Place and a Part of Routes

We can think of a congregation's meeting space and those it assembles narrowly as a particular place. Indeed, the very meaning of *congregation* involves being a gathering, which is a core characteristic of place. We can ask this assembly in place the attending questions I offered earlier in chapters 6 and 7. What is gathered in this congregation? How does it gather its members as individuals? What emotional connections exist with the congregation (levels of empathy, experiences of belonging and alienation, etc.)? What social, interpersonal, intrapersonal, and ecological dynamics in this congregation help or hinder the flourishing of life and the Spirit? How is God at work in this congregation and calling its members into partnership?

Congregations in Place and among Routes (Living as Parish)

We can think of a congregation more broadly as including its larger context and within a network of places connected by routes. In this regard, we think in terms of how the congregation belongs to and serves the place it exists. This is a reclamation of understanding congregations as *parishes*—geographic areas of ecclesial care. Interestingly, the roots of the word *parish* go back to Greek terms for "neighbor/neighboring" (dwelling with others) and "sojourning" (traveling on routes).[13] So we can shift the focus of attending questions for places and routes from the congregation to its parish. What is gathered in this parish? How does this parish gather its inhabitants as individuals? What emotional connections exist between the congregation and this parish (levels of empathy, experiences of belonging and alienation, etc.)? What social, interpersonal, intrapersonal, and ecological dynamics in this parish help and hinder the flourishing of life and the Spirit? How is God at work in this parish and calling its members and this congregation into partnership?

Congregational Ministries and Vocation-in-Place

Congregations are places of vocation *and* places equipping for vocation-in-place. As such, congregations gather their members in collective vocation to their parishes but also equip and send members into partnership with God in the places they dwell and on the routes they travel. Sometimes leaders ponder how they can get laity involved in the ministry of the church. This is a good question, but it can also limit vocational imagination. Just as we should not locate vocation solely within the work of pastors and professionals, we should not equate the programmatic ministries of congregations with the vocation of the laity. We must think about the gathered ministries of congregations *and* the distributed ministries of the laity. It is an age-old rhythm of gathering and scattering the body of Christ in the world.

So we must attend to how congregations equip persons individually and collectively for vocation-in-place. What does the congregation *explicitly* teach about vocation-in-place? What does the congregation *implicitly* teach about vocation-in-place? On what aspects about vocation-in-place is the congregation silent?

GOALS OF EQUIPPING FOR VOCATION-IN-PLACE

The goals of ministries that equip persons for vocation-in-place are interwoven with the goals of discipleship ministries. Deepening our abilities to be in Christian vocation-in-place depends on formation in the way of Jesus. Companionship with Jesus comingles with partnership in God's work in the world. To know is to do—to do is to know. To know the way of Jesus is to do the work of Jesus—to do the work of Jesus is to know the way of Jesus.

The following goals focus on fostering vocation-in-place but should be considered in conjunction with goals of discipleship ministries:

- Integrate vocational and discipleship ministries in all the seasons of life.

- Foster understanding of how the congregation and its larger tradition views God's work in the world. To be in partnership with God, individuals and communities need some sense of what God is doing in the world. Developing this sense will entail holding in creative tension a variety of perspectives (e.g., Great Commission, Great Commandment, Kin-dom of God, Micah 6:8).

- Develop awareness of vocation as continually evolving and rooted in the places and routes of life.

- Fuel the imagination of persons and groups to see themselves as being in vocation.

- Provide resources and skills for knowing the place of the parish and routes in and through it.

- Instill personal capacities for partnership with God such as the fruit of the Spirit and those presented in chapter 5—faith, hope, love, integrity, agency, and mutuality.

- Nurture empathy, openness, and courage that allow freedom to be responsive to God's call.

- Develop capacities to engage in vocational theology:

  a. Recognizing the connections we have with place

  b. Identifying who and what is gathered by places and routes

  c. Naming ways places and routes gather us

    d. Exploring how the relationships in places and on routes help and hinder flourishing of life and the Spirit

    e. Partnering with God's place-making and way-making work

As these goals shape ministries' equipping for vocation-in-place, we can look for several indicators of growing vocational imagination:

- Attentiveness to the dynamics and practices of gathering

- A sense of connectedness with the places and journeys of life

- Attention to the intersections of human and ecological graces and brokenness in places

- Service that is intergenerational and inclusive of all abilities

- Diversity of gifts and graces embodied in a variety of forms of partnership with God

- Shared stories of faith and vocation

- A sense of constant support, value, and commissioning that persons in congregations experience for vocation-in-place[14]

- Awareness of vocation in both the present moment and openness to future ways of being in vocation

- A deepening respond-ability to God—that is, growth in sanctification

FOSTERING VOCATION-IN-PLACE

Congregations are already doing a great deal to foster spiritual growth and service through worship and mission ministries. Some congregations use a formal discipleship program (e.g., The United Methodist Church's *See All the People*) to help persons connect faith with daily life. Some congregations emphasize themes such as *What Would Jesus Do? (WWJD)*, Robert Schnase's *Five Practices of Fruitful Congregations*,[15] or Rick Warren's *Purpose Driven Church*.[16] Other congregations may implement a version of a spiritual gifts inventory and facilitate matching gifts to ministries.

Each of these can make valuable contributions to discipleship and a sense of vocation.

Two caveats need consideration in building on such approaches to foster vocation-in-place. The first is that these approaches root vocation in the individual and fail to address the role of place in vocation. Certainly, we must attend to the uniqueness of individual vocation in the places and on the routes of life. However, to stop there is only a partial engagement of vocation. Places and routes call us, even claim us, in ways suggesting that vocation is rooted in places and routes. Just as we might use tools of discerning personal giftedness (and brokenness), we must use tools of discerning the giftedness (and brokenness) of places and routes.

The second caveat is that the above approaches tend to function as programs. Fostering a sense of vocational imagination takes more than programming; it requires intentional systemic formation. Imagination, much like faith itself, is a way of perceiving the world—something akin to a worldview. "Place" is the way we imagine the web of relationships in particular areas and the relationship between God and the world in those areas. "Vocation" is the way we imagine God's relationship with the world, God's work in the midst of the world, and ways to partner with God's work. Programs can provide beliefs and practices, but these are only resources for faith and vocational imagination. To form faith and vocational imagination, we need to experience a formational system, an educational ecology.[17] This is analogous to learning a language. One can take any number of classes to learn a second language and become proficient communicating in that language. However, it takes some kind of immersion in a context shaped by that language to become fluent to the point of thinking in that language and no longer translating between languages. Focusing on programs is like assuming language classes will create a native speaker, when at best they produce proficient translators. To foster the kind of vocation-in-place presented here, we must work with congregational cultures and their formational systems to create immersive contexts. Such contexts form imagination for partnership with God and hearts empathetic to others. We must attend to how we gather the saints—how we form relationships with the saints through the stories we tell and the practices of the formational system.

Stories We Tell

Stories shape our imagination as we hear them and allow ourselves to enter into them, exploring what it might be like to be in their world. The stories of a community are also resources for constructing our own individual stories. Communal stories offer possible story lines for how we construct ourselves from the collection of our discreet past experiences. Congregations and denominations hold several genres of stories: conversions, testimonies, faith journeys, roads to recovery, dark nights of the soul, healings, and callings.

The robustness of vocation among the members of a faith community is a function of the richness of vocational (call) stories held and valued (authorized) in that community. This richness involves the range of vocations portrayed and range of vocational forms each story conveys. The range of vocations depicted stems from the following:

- Stories of models and mentors (the "saints") past and present

- Stories from diverse age levels, maturity of faith, and abilities

- Stories from diverse groups of people (ethnicity, gender, sexuality, class, denominations, religions, etc.)

- Stories from clergy, congregational staff, and laity

- The messages vocational stories portray

- How one recognizes and discerns vocation

- The role of place and routes in evoking vocation

- What God is seeking to do in the world

- Ways that persons respond to callings of God in place and on routes

- Forms that vocation may take

- Who may be in vocation

- Challenges and aides to being in vocation

In conversations with students after they return writing assignments about faith journeys and place, I frequently hear about the helpfulness of the process. I am surprised how often students say they have never been asked or given the opportunity to tell their story. The power of stories to form vocational imagination is lost if opportunities to tell and hear these stories in faith communities do not exist.

Stories author identity and vocation for good and ill. The vocational stories a congregation tells, neglects, and suppresses various forms of vocation. Vocational imagination is not value neutral. The power of vocational stories warrants ethical and theological scrutiny.

Formational System

Maria Harris argues that the church does not *have* an educational ministry—it *is* an educational ministry.[18] From this perspective, we can think of a congregation's formative system or educational ecology in terms of the following:

- Worship, sacraments, and liturgy (continually confirming and commissioning daily vocation)

- Times of community

- Communication channels (newsletters, bulletins, websites, social media)

- Stories and testimony

- Instruction and intentional learning opportunities

- Mission, service, and outreach[19]

A congregation's educational ecology forms individuals and groups in many aspects of faith and discipleship. We must see in these systems not only discipleship formation but formation for vocation-in-place as well. Specifically, we need to be conscious of the explicit and implicit ways the educational ecology shapes imagination about vocation-in-place and equips persons with knowledge, skills, and emotions to embody vocation-in-place.

Develop Attentiveness to Place

One avenue for equipping for vocation-in-place is to engage the movements for attending to place and routes presented earlier:

- Developing empathy through astuteness about our emotional closeness and distance with our places and routes

- Providing resources to name and describe what and who is gathered in a place and on a route

- Fostering skills of self-awareness and honesty about how our places and routes shape us for good and ill

- Creating prophetic insight about what shapes relationships in our places and routes and how these foster and hinder flourishing of life and the Spirit

- Empowering partnership with God's place-making and way-making

Foster Practices

A second avenue for equipping for vocation-in-place is to foster practices that connect us constructively with places and routes. Such practices both make someone or something present to us and relational to us. They create relational presence.

- Hearing into speech creates a space where voice (and with it one's sense of self) comes into being. Hearing others and creation deeply is more than the active listening technique of effective communication. The voice and self of the other become present and relatable.

- Seeing into visibility creates a space where one's self and soul become embodied. This kind of seeing is not voyeurism, exposure of the other, or merely recognizing the body of the other. Rather, an embodied self—a self-incarnate—becomes present and relatable.

- Feeling into empathy creates a space where the experiences of others become accessible. This kind of feeling is not pity, nor is it projection of experience onto another. The experiences of others become present and relatable.

These practices mingle as the practice of love of God, neighbor, and creation. By creating relational presence, they also make it possible for what and who we encounter in place and on routes to claim and call us.

Remove Obstacles

A third avenue for equipping for vocation-in-place is to remove obstacles. Sometimes our most important work in fostering vocation-in-place is removing the obstacles of systemic sin hindering responsiveness to and partnership with God. A historical example is how sexism limited the leadership roles of women in the church and prevented ordination. The church has also historically struggled with embracing the contributions of youth as "youth" and not as "the future church." More recently, segments of the church are becoming aware of attitudes and obstacles impeding the vocations of persons with disabilities. Many denominations and congregations are deeply divided about embracing the vocations of LGBTQ persons. Racism within and beyond the church discounts and rejects the capacities of persons of color to be in vocation-in-place. Removing obstacles to vocation-in-place is not a matter of inclusiveness—it is a matter of not getting in the way of a call from God and place and a person's response to that call. Impeding that call is not just being a hindrance, but by virtue of interfering with the will of God, it is sin.

GATHERING SAINTS

On All Saints' Day, many congregations honor mentors and models in faith. The lives of these persons resource and inspire our imaginations about what it means to shaped by the love of God and responsive to the call of God in place. We gather the saints every day and not just on All Saints'. Every day we gather in the present the saints of today and the saints of the past. As Alfred North Whitehead points out,

> The communion of saints is a great and inspiring assemblage, but it has
> only one possible hall of meeting, and that is, the present, and the mere

lapse of time through which any particular group of saints must travel to reach that meeting-place, makes very little difference.[20]

The assemblage of the saints is ever expanding, and as it grows we are ushered into the future—into the constant calling of God in place and on routes of life. Imagining oneself as part of the saints may be hard to accept because we think of saints as perfect and we know we fall short of that high bar. However, to be part of that communion is more about commitment to partner with God in the world (holiness) than being perfect (purity). Part of the place-making vocation of religious leaders is gathering and forming the saints.

FOR REFLECTION

Personal Perspective

1. What is your practical theology of place at this point? What are its key convictions, assumptions, and practices?

2. In what ways does place prove helpful in understanding vocation and ministry dynamics in various contexts?

3. In light of the emphasis on places and routes evoking vocation, how do you think about being called and relocating to a place?

4. How have people, communities, places, and routes shaped your vocational imagination? . . . equipped you for vocation-in-place and vocation-en-route?

5. In what ways do you practice hearing into speech, beholding into visibility, and feeling into empathy as part place-making and way-making?

Leadership Perspective

6. How does your practical theology of place shape your work as leader and educator? . . . your sense of vocation in the place you lead and educate?

7. To what extent do you equate the ministry of a faith community with the programs and initiatives of the congregation? How can the vocations of the members scattered throughout the week become visible and seen as the ministry of the church?

8. Review your goals for fostering discipleship and vocation. Whether or not you agree with the positions presented in this book, what ideas help you evaluate these goals?

9. Review the ways you form and equip persons for vocation-in-place and vocation-en-route. Whether or not you agree with the positions presented in this book, what ideas help you evaluate your approach and efforts?

10. What obstacles to vocation do you most often work to remove?

Congregational Perspective

11. How would you describe the congregation's sense of collective vocation?

12. What shapes the vocational imagination of the congregation? What fuels it and hinders it?

13. Map all the various activities of the congregation (worship, committees, small groups, classes, programs, communications, etc.). What do these activities individually and collectively contribute to forming and equipping people for vocation-in-place and vocation-en route?

14. In what ways does the congregation practice hearing into speech, beholding into visibility, and feeling into empathy as part their vocation and life together?

NOTES

Preface

1. Mary McClintock Fulkerson, *Places of Redemption: Theology for a Worldly Church* (Oxford: Oxford University Press, 2010).

2. Ibid., 26.

3. Dr. Linda Mercandante, a colleague at MTSO, reports that during her research for *Belief without Borders: Inside the Minds of the Spiritual but Not Religious* (Oxford: Oxford University Press, 2014) she found many people with those characteristics within Christian congregations.

4. Jack Seymour, *Teaching the Way of Jesus* (Nashville: Abingdon Press, 2014), 84.

Chapter One

1. Stephen Crites, "The Narrative Quality of Experience," *Journal of the American Academy of Religion* 39, no. 3 (Sep. 1971): 291–311.

2. James Fowler, *Becoming Adult: Becoming Christian* (San Francisco: Jossey-Bass, 2000), 75.

3. Attributed to Ada María Isasi-Díaz, "Kin-dom" emphasizes the just relationships in God's reign in contrast to the patriarchal rule of territory that *kingdom* connotes. *Kin-dom* is an apt term in this project, since place is an arena of meaningful relationships rather than a controlled space. See Ada María Isasi-Díaz, *En La Lucha* (Minneapolis: Fortress Press, 2004), 4.

4. Jack Seymour identifies signs of this work as the blind see, the crippled walk, diseases are healed, the deaf hear, the dead are raised, the

poor hear good news, and the prisoners are freed. These actions bring social wholeness as well: "Restoring community or building community is therefore at the heart of God's realm and of the healings of Jesus. Restoring community is also true for those who ask for forgiveness. Relationships are built." Jack Seymour, *Teaching the Way of Jesus* (Nashville: Abingdon Press, 2014), 132–33. My project complements the work of Seymour in *Teaching the Way of Jesus, Yearning for God* (with Margaret Ann Crain), and *Educating Christians* (with Margaret Ann Crain and Joseph Crockett).

5. Yi-Fu Tuan, *Topophilia: A Study of Environmental Perception, Attitudes, and Values* (New York: Columbia University Press, 1974), 93.

6. Tim Cresswell, *Place: An Introduction* (Chichester: Wiley-Blackwell, 2015), 35.

Chapter Two

1. "Hear, O Israel: The Lord is our God, the Lord alone. You shall love the Lord your God with all your heart, and with all your soul, and with all your might" (Deut 6:4-5).

2. See Jack Seymour, *Teaching the Way of Jesus* (Nashville: Abingdon Press, 2014), 77–81 regarding the markers of Jesus's ministry of the Realm of God that point to rebuilding community.

3. Flourishing leads to fruits. The fruit of the Spirit is found in Galatians 5:22-23: "By contrast, the fruit of the Spirit is love, joy, peace, patience, kindness, generosity, faithfulness, gentleness, and self-control."

4. We can also see this in the use of apocalyptic literature. This literature is written for the oppressed, but in the hands of those in power, it can be used to demonize them.

5. In Wesleyan traditions, these forms of grace are framed as prevenient, justifying, and sanctifying grace.

6. Halvor Moxnes, "Identity in Jesus' Galilee—From Ethnicity to Locative Intersectionality," *Biblical Interpretation* 18 (2010): 392.

7. Yvette Murphy et al., *Incorporating Intersectionality in Social Work Practice, Research, Policy, and Education* (Washington, DC: National As-

sociation of Social Workers Press, 2009), 7. The impact of the womanist movement is extremely influential in the development of intersectionality thinking.

8. Mike Parent, Cirleen DeBlaere, and Bonnie Moradi, "Approaches to Research on Intersectionality: Perspectives on Gender, LGBT, and Racial/Ethnic Identities," *Sex Roles* 68, nos. 11–12 (2013): 640.

9. Michele Tracy Berger and Kathleen Guidroz, *The Intersectional Approach: Transforming the Academy through Race, Class, and Gender* (Chapel Hill: University of North Carolina Press, 2009), 7.

10. Here I am specifically dealing with the socio-ecological brokenness. Psycho-spiritual brokenness in the individual also fractures vocational imagination leading to choices to reject God's invitation and call.

11. See Mary McClintock Fulkerson, *Places of Redemption: Theology for a Worldly Church* (New York: Oxford University Press, 2007), 17–25 regarding obliviousness.

12. William Bean Kennedy, "The Ideological Captivity of the Non-Poor," in *Pedagogies for the Non-Poor*, ed. Alice Frazer Evans, Robert A. Evans, and William Bean Kennedy (Maryknoll, NY: Orbis Books, 1987), 237.

13. For an argument for a place-making agenda, see David A. Gruenewald's "Foundations of Place: A Multidisciplinary Framework for Place-Conscious Education," in *American Educational Research Journal* 40, no. 3 (Fall 2003): 619–54.

14. This is not freedom from place. One is emerging from what place gathers, so we are always conditioned by place, but that does not mean we must be determined by it.

15. "As human beings continue to enhance their power to manipulate and destroy ecosystems and cultures, it may not be too much of a stretch to claim that place making has become the ultimate human vocation. Ultimately, the kinds of places that we acknowledge and make possible will determine the kinds and the quality of human and nonhuman life in our communities, bioregions, and on our planet. This prospect suggests an

active role for schools as centers of both inquiry and action in local, re-gional, and global space" (Gruenewald, "Foundations of Place," 636–37).

Chapter Three

1. "Tradition is not fixed for all time; on the other hand, it is not com-pletely subject to historical vicissitudes. It is the perpetuation of a chang-ing, developing identity. Tradition is the living faith of the dead; tradition-alism is the dead faith of the living. Tradition lives in conversation with the past, while remembering we are where and when we are and that it is we who have to decide. Traditionalism supposes that nothing should ever be done for the first time." Joseph Carey, "Christianity as an Enfolding Circle [conversation with Jaroslav Pelikan]," *U.S. News and World Report*, June 26, 1989, 57. A related theme exists in Alasdair MacIntyre's notion that a tradition is an extended argument over time. Alasdair MacIntyre, *Whose Justice? Which Rationality?* (Notre Dame, IN: University of Notre Dame Press, 1988), 12.

2. There came an important time for those who first journeyed with Jesus when he called them "friends" rather than slaves because they knew what he was about (John 15:15). Up to that point, their discipleship was defined by following; now, Jesus shifts the emphasis in discipleship to partnership with God's work in the world.

3. John Westerhoff III, *Will Our Children Have Faith?* (Harrisburg, PA: Morehouse Publishing, 2000), 87.

4. James Fowler, *Stages of Faith: The Psychology of Human Development and the Quest for Meaning* (New York: Harper and Row, 1981), 91.

5. Frederick Buechner, *Wishful Thinking: A Theological ABC* (New York: Harper and Row, 1973), 95.

6. Vocation is an important theme in Christian religious education. See Jack Seymour, *Teaching the Way of Jesus* (Nashville: Abingdon Press, 2014); Anne Streaty Wimberly, *Soul Stories* (Nashville: Abingdon Press, 2005); Margaret Ann Crain and Jack Seymour, *Yearning for God* (Nash-ville: Upper Room, 2003); Jack L. Seymour, Margaret Ann Crain, and Jo-seph V. Crockett, *Educating Christians* (Nashville: Abingdon Press, 1993); Mary Elizabeth Moore, *Teaching as a Sacramental Act* (Cleveland: Pilgrim,

2004); Norma Cook Everist, *The Church as Learning Community* (Nashville: Abingdon Press, 2002).

7. James Fowler, *Becoming Adult, Becoming Christian: Adult Development and Christian Faith* (San Francisco: Harper and Row, 1984), 95.

8. James Fowler, *Weaving the New Creation* (San Francisco: Harper, 1991), 121. This definition seems to assume that vocation is something one has and one needs to find a setting in which to express and embody it.

9. Thanks to Dr. Lisa Withrow of Methodist Theological School in Ohio for this insight.

10. As introduced in chapter 1.

Chapter Four

1. See chapter 1 for the development of this idea.

2. Edward Casey, *Getting Back into Place*, 2nd ed. (Bloomington: Indiana University Press, 2009), 327–28.

3. Ibid., 329.

4. Ibid., xxv.

5. Tim Cresswell, *Place: An Introduction* (Chichester: Wiley-Blackwell, 2015), 19.

6. Ibid., 18.

7. Ibid., 70–71.

8. Jeff Malpas, *Place and Experience: A Philosophy of Topography* (Cambridge: Cambridge University Press, 1999), 35.

9. Qtd. in Mary McClintock Fulkerson, *Places of Redemption: Theology for a Worldly Church* (Oxford: Oxford University Press, 2010), 35. Fulkerson is quoting Pierre Bourdieu, formative theorist on the nature of practice.

10. Cresswell, *Place*, 68.

11. Ibid., 42.

12. Ibid., 47.

13. "Heaven," performed by The Talking Heads on the CD *Fear of Music* (Sire Records: 1979).

14. Cresswell, *Place*, 70–71.

15. See Doreen Massey's chapter "A Global Sense of Place" (particularly page 151) in Doreen Massey, *Space, Place, and Gender* (Minneapolis: University of Minnesota Press, 1994).

16. Again, see Massey, "A Global Sense of Place" and Cresswell, *Place*, 62–65.

17. Examples include Craig Bartholomew, *Where Mortals Dwell: A Christian View of Place for Today* (Grand Rapids, MI: Baker Academic, 2011); John Inge, *A Christian Theology of Place* (Aldershot: Ashgate, 2003); Sarah Morice-Brubaker, *The Place of the Spirit: Toward a Trinitarian Theology of Location* (Eugene, OR: Pickwick, 2013).

18. See Walter Brueggemann, *The Land: Place as Gift, Promise, and Challenge in Biblical Faith* (Minneapolis: Augsburg, 2002).

19. "We know that the whole creation has been groaning in labor pains until now; and not only the creation, but we ourselves, who have the first fruits of the Spirit, groan inwardly while we wait for adoption, the redemption of our bodies" (Rom 8:22-23).

Chapter Five

1. Stephen Crites, "The Narrative Quality of Experience," *Journal of the American Academy of Religion* 39, no. 3 (Sep. 1971): 291–311.

2. Romans 12:6-8: prophecy, ministry, teaching, exhortation, generosity, leadership, compassion. 1 Corinthians 12:4-11: wisdom, knowledge, faith, healing, working of miracles, prophecy, discernment, speaking in tongues, interpretation of tongues. 1 Corinthians 12:28: deeds of power, gifts of healing, forms of assistance, forms of leadership, various kinds of tongues.

3. "Love, joy, peace, patience, kindness, generosity, faithfulness, gentleness, and self-control" (Gal 5:22-23).

4. See "accrued confidence" as part of Erik Erikson's Identity vs. Role Confusion developmental stage. Erik Erikson, *Childhood and Society* (New York: Norton, 1993), 261.

5. An allusion to Romans 12:1.

6. There are a wide range of reasons for why people may not have the freedom to move: lack of resources, coercion, oppression, disability, addiction, fear, or commitments to others.

7. "There is no fear in love, but perfect love casts out fear; for fear has to do with punishment, and whoever fears has not reached perfection in love" (1 John 4:18).

8. "For I am convinced that neither death, nor life, nor angels, nor rulers, nor things present, nor things to come, nor powers, nor height, nor depth, nor anything else in all creation, will be able to separate us from the love of God in Christ Jesus our Lord" (Rom 8:38-39).

9. See Parker Palmer, *The Courage to Teach: Exploring the Inner Landscape of a Teacher's Life* (San Francisco: Jossey-Bass, 2007).

10. See Mary Elizabeth Moore, *Education for Continuity and Change* (Nashville: Abingdon Press, 1983).

11. As we think about the relationship between self and place, it is easy to fall prey to false dichotomies between them. Dichotomous thinking asks if the self creates place or if place creates self; if an individual transforms place or place transforms individuals; if we give or receive from place. We need to think in terms of the self and place as co-creative. *I Am—Place* creates self and place at the same time.

12. This relates to the argument of Carol Gilligan that moral development in girls is more narrative than logical-mathematical, as tends to be the case in boys. See Carol Gilligan, *In a Different Voice: Psychological Theory and Women's Development* (Cambridge, MA: Harvard University Press, 1982).

175

13. "So if anyone is in Christ, there is a new creation: everything old has passed away; see, everything has become new!" (2 Cor 5:17)

14. Children who have several such sets of Legos before long borrow among them for expanded possibilities of creativity. This analogy may also be fitting for ways we borrow from traditions not our own.

15. Jack Seymour and Margaret Ann Crain write that in mainline denominations members miss out on being authored and authorized in vocation because they are rarely given opportunities to tell their stories. See Crain and Seymour, *Yearning for God: Reflections of Faithful Lives* (Nashville: Upper Room, 2003).

16. A powerful educational model of this is Anne Streaty Wimberly's "story-linking" approach described in *Soul Stories: African American Christian Education* (Nashville: Abingdon Press, 2005).

17. Tradition and scripture are not listed in this mix directly because they are the resources informing these understandings. Drawing on scripture, tradition, and the Spirit is part of the processes of discipleship and formation.

Chapter Six

1. My thinking about the role of affect in relation to place is informed by the work of Jacqui Buschor, an MDiv student at Methodist Theological School in Ohio.

2. This can also include particular personal places within these dwellings, such as prayer corners, gardens, man caves, and so forth.

3. Robert K. Barnhart, ed., "Belong," *Chambers Dictionary of Etymology* (New York: Chambers, 1988), 88.

4. *Which* is not the same question as *whether* God is calling us *to* this place.

5. See Simone Weil's development of the idea that study (deep attentiveness) is prayer in her essay "Reflections on the Right Use of School Studies with a View to the Love of God," in *Simone Weil: Selected Writings* (Maryknoll, NY: Orbis Books, 1998).

6. An interesting question is whether a resume is a listing of personal achievements and thus is regarded as private property or a listing of graces bestowed by a community/place and thus has an element of being communal property.

7. See Nelle Morton, *The Journey Is Home* (Boston: Beacon, 1985), 127–29.

8. See McClintock Fulkerson's discussion of obliviousness and appearing. Mary McClintock Fulkerson, *Places of Redemption: Theology for a Worldly Church* (New York: Oxford University Press, 2007), 21.

9. Partnership is not always action. It also involves a passive aspect that allows for receiving, waiting, being present, and just showing up.

10. I think we can faithfully proclaim this as Christians without dismissing religious traditions whose practices share aspects of the way of Jesus.

Chapter Seven

1. See Nelle Morton, *The Journey Is Home* (Boston: Beacon, 1985).

2. Tim Cresswell, *Place: An Introduction* (Chichester: Wiley-Blackwell, 2015), 63–64.

3. Mihály Csíkszentmihályi, *Flow: The Psychology of Optimal Experience* (New York: Harper Perennial, 2008).

4. This idea was suggested by Jacqui Buschor, MDiv student at Methodist Theological School in Ohio.

5. The issue here is objectification, not enjoyment of cross-cultural engagement, nor traveling to broaden awareness of the world.

6. Some routes are indeed dangerous, but the issue here is making the Other a de facto threat.

7. Parker Palmer, *The Courage to Teach* (San Francisco: Jossey-Bass, 1998), 57.

8. So often we create a great deal of waste (particularly packaging) in order to make our belongings, food, and drink portable.

9. Partnership is not always action; it is also receiving, waiting, being present, and showing up. Partnership in the present is connected with vocation in the past and anticipated vocation.

Chapter Eight

1. See Don S. Browning, *A Fundamental Practical Theology* (Minneapolis: Fortress, 1991).

2. See Thomas Groome, *Christian Religious Education* (San Francisco: Jossey-Bass, 1999), and Thomas Groome, *Sharing Faith* (San Francisco: Harper, 1991).

3. See Daniel Patte, *Ethics of Biblical Interpretation: A Reevaluation* (Louisville, KY: Westminster John Knox, 1995).

4. Edward Farley, "Interpreting Situations: An Inquiry into the Nature of Practical Theology," in *The Blackwell Reader in Pastoral and Practical Theology*, ed. James Woodward and Stephen Pattison (Malden, MA: Blackwell, 2000), 119–20.

5. Mary McClintock Fulkerson, *Places of Redemption: Theology for a Worldly Church* (New York: Oxford University Press, 2007), 28.

6. Ibid., 32.

7. Ibid., 26.

8. Ibid. Italics in original.

9. Ibid., 51.

10. Ibid., 27.

11. Ibid., 40.

12. "In the framework of this analysis practical theology has a special form because it addresses, *thematizes vocation as a situation*. Because ministry is itself a situation, it presupposes and needs practical theology

in its fundamental sense of a hermeneutic of situations, but moves beyond that to the special requirements of the vocational situation" (Farley, "Interpreting Situations," 122. Emphasis added). See also Bonnie Miller-McLemore's metaphor for thinking of situations as "the living human web" in Bonnie Miller-McLemore, "The Living Human Web: Pastoral Theology at the Turn of the Century," in *Through the Eyes of Women: Insights for Pastoral Care*, ed. Jeanne Stevenson Moessner (Minneapolis: Fortress, 1996), 9–26.

13. Robert K. Barnhart, ed., "Parish," *Chamber's Dictionary of Etymology* (New York: Chambers, 1988), 757.

14. See Norma Cook Everist, *The Church as Learning Community* (Nashville: Abingdon Press, 2002) particularly chapter 8.

15. Robert Schnase, *Five Practices of Fruitful Congregations* (Nashville: Abingdon Press, 2007).

16. Rick Warren, *Purpose Driven Church* (Grand Rapids, MI: Zondervan, 1995).

17. See in particular Maria Harris, *Fashion Me a People* (Louisville, KY: Westminster John Knox, 1989), and Charles Foster, *From Generation to Generation* (Eugene, OR: Cascade Books, 2012).

18. Harris, *Fashion Me a People*. See also Mary Elizabeth Mullino Moore, *Teaching as a Sacramental Act* (Cleveland: Pilgrim, 2004)

19. Largely informed by Harris, *Fashion Me a People*.

20. Alfred North Whitehead, *The Aims of Education and Other Essays* (New York: Free Press, 1967), 3.

CPSIA information can be obtained
at www.ICGtesting.com
Printed in the USA
LVHW041938280219
609120LV00002B/11